Murder

in

Harrill Hills

by R. S. Allen

∞INFINITY
PUBLISHING

ISBN 978-0-7414-6546-7 Paperback
ISBN 978-0-7414-9404-7 eBook

Printed in the United States of America

Published December 2012

INFINITY PUBLISHING
1094 New DeHaven Street, Suite 100
West Conshohocken, PA 19428-2713
Toll-free (877) BUY BOOK
Local Phone (610) 941-9999
Fax (610) 941-9959
Info@buybooksontheweb.com
www.buybooksontheweb.com

Other non-fiction books by R. S. Allen

Schoolboy: Jim Tugerson: Ace of the '53 Smokies,
Infinity Publishing, September, 2008
ISBN 0-7414-4986-2

The Perry's Camp Murders (with Steve O. Watson),
Infinity Publishing, August, 2009
ISBN 0-7414-5528-5

In Memory of
Mary Tabler Hankins

CONTENTS

"The dead cannot cry out for justice; it is a duty of the living to do so for them."

- Bujold, *Diplomatic Immunity,* 2002

INTRODUCTION

The year was 1951. Things were very different then in Knoxville and throughout East Tennessee. Most people worked forty hours a week and worked overtime on a weekday or Saturday, not Sunday. Sunday was reserved for attending church and worshiping God. Few businesses were even open on Sunday. Christianity was a part of most everyone's lives.

No homes had television since the first Knoxville television station did not broadcast until October 1953. Rotary-dial telephones were still for the most part on a party line with neighbors. All the cars were built in Detroit and were built by Ford, General Motors, or Chrysler. A "foreign car" was just that – foreign.

The Super Bowl and "March Madness" were not yet a part of the national vocabulary, but everyone knew what was meant when "The Fall Classic" was mentioned. In March "All About Eve" won the Oscar for Best Picture of 1950, but one of the most popular films making the rounds in East Tennessee theaters was Tennessee's untelevised Cotton Bowl victory over Texas.

It was a time when no one locked their doors or feared for their children to play outside from morning to night.

It was also a time when young people that had grown up in a rural community would seek employment in the city. Such was the case of Mary Tabler. She grew up in the Corryton community of Knox County, a community inhabited by God-fearing, church-going folks who mostly farmed for a living. There were a couple of country stores in the community, but to find items not stocked on these stores' shelves, everyone had to travel down the road to Fountain City, an unincorporated community in Knox County just north of Knoxville.

After finishing high school Mary went to work for Standard Knitting Mills, one of the largest employers in Knoxville at the time. She would work in the mills' office and perform secretarial duties for the next ten years. She would take enough time out in 1946 to marry her high school sweetheart – C. Fred Hankins – whom she had known all her life.

Mary would continue to work at her secretarial job while Fred continued to develop his lumber contracting business. They would settle in the Fountain City area and would design and build the house of their dreams in the Harrill Hills section of Fountain City in 1950, moving into the new home in November in time for Thanksgiving.

At the end of March 1951, however, tragedy would strike the Hankins and Tabler families in such a way that things would never be as they had been. While Fred was gone that Saturday afternoon to get some work done on their car and to wile away some time at his father's furniture business, Mary allowed an intruder to enter their home, an intruder who would shoot the life out of her before she could escape his grasp. Fred would return home to find her dying, and she would, in fact, be dead within the hour.

In short order, their new home was consumed with neighbors, ambulance attendants, officers from the Knox County Sheriff's Office, the coroner, family members, reporters from both Knoxville newspapers, but no one among them could explain how or why this had happened. There was no explanation, motive, or suspects. Nothing about this heinous murder made any sense.

There would be rampant speculation and rumors but no evidence. Numerous suspects would be questioned and released. There would only be two suspects of any consequence, and the first of these was almost two years away. This suspect would be arrested prematurely, arrested before his ironclad alibi was checked, and he would be released among a throng of sympathizers and well wishers.

The second suspect of consequence was almost four years away and compelling circumstantial evidence would be developed against him but not enough to charge him with the murder. The Knox County Attorney General wanted a confession from this cocky prison-hardened criminal but the confession never came, and this prime suspect lived 31 years longer than Mary Hankins.

Such a crime was not indicative of those times or of the neighborhood where it occurred. The only thing that was indicative of the times was Mrs. Hankins' funeral. A throng of mourners came to the Graveston Baptist Church in Corryton, the church where Mary and Fred had grown up, and where she had been a Sunday school teacher.

These grief-stricken mourners – husband, family members, and friends from work and the community – were there with two one-word questions rolling over and over in their minds. These words were, of course, "Why?" and "Who?" This funeral was the type where people cried, fainted, and spoke out loud to the deceased. Sadly, there were also the curious among the mourners – "the lookers" – as described by a family member - were people who had never met Mrs. Hankins.

The pages that follow are intended to answer the "who" and the "why" in the minds of the mourners rather than the curiosity of "the lookers."

Most of the information for this book was found in newspaper archives. Unfortunately, the investigative files of the Knox County Sherriff's Office concerning the Hankins murder no longer exist. In the 1950s it was accepted practice for investigators to maintain their own files, take them home with them or wherever they wanted. As a result the files disappeared in time, usually after the investigator retired or died. None of the investigators who worked on this case are still alive, but fortunately there are a few who knew them and who learned of details that survived the demise of the investigators and the files' contents.

A cropped head shot of the following photograph is the only photograph ever published in *The Knoxville Journal* or *The Knoxville News-Sentinel* that accompanied any information concerning Mrs. Hankins' murder. It became as familiar to those who followed the case at the time as the Hankins name itself. This photograph was taken on her wedding day, November 10, 1946, four and one-half years before her death. The photograph of her husband, Fred, depicted in the first chapter was also taken on the day they wed. A cropped version of this photograph also appeared in the Knoxville papers.

Mary Hankins

CHAPTER 1

A GRIEVOUS, LIFE-ENDING DAY

The last day of Mary Hankins' life – Saturday, March 31, 1951 – was a cool, crisp Spring day, but not too cool to work outside. Mary and her husband, Fred, had been outside working together during the early part of the day, and there was plenty of work for them to do.

The Hankins had moved into their new brick home situated at the corner of Forest Lane and Crestwood Road in Fountain City's Harrill Hills in time for Thanksgiving less than five months earlier. Harrill Hills was a fashionable neighborhood where stylish homes were still being built by young middle class Knoxville couples. They had moved from a home on Highland Drive in the Inskip community – the western most edge of Fountain City.

The holidays and winter had delayed landscaping and putting in a yard, but the Hankins were anxious to get started. Piles of construction dirt still awaited removal or spreading around the Hankins home.

Fred Hankins was vice-president of Construction Services Company, Incorporated, located next door to Chavannes Lumber Company where he had previously worked as a salesman, in the 500 block of West Oldham Avenue. The lumber yard was near the southern end of Southern Railway's Coster Shops, the railroad company's maintenance and repair facility. This business location no longer exists, having disappeared in the 1960's with the construction of Interstate 75, and later with expanded construction of Interstate 275 connecting the north and sound bound Interstate 75 and the east and west bound Interstate 40.

Fred was in the business of building roofs and as a result was very knowledgeable about building houses. Consequently, he had contracted the building of their new Harrill Hills home. He and Mary had put their own touches into the design of the house. They had included a basement with a side door entry from the driveway and garage. The house had been seated diagonally at the corner of Forest Lane and Crestwood Road but the house had a Forest Lane address as the driveway ran off Forest, not Crestwood.

The Hankins House 2010

There was a neighbor immediately next door on Crestwood, but not on Forest. The houses on the next road over, Dogwood Road, were further away than either of the nearest homes on Crestwood. Fred's parents, James E. and Bell Hankins, lived on Briarcliff Road, a couple of roads away in the other direction.

Building this home was one of the most exciting times of their life together. Because of this excitement there were things going on in the world outside their domestic realm that either hardly noticed.

Since moving into their new home, William Faulkner had won a Nobel Prize for Literature; Paul Harvey had begun his national radio broadcast; the Tennessee Vols had won a National Championship in football by virtue of a 20-14 win over Texas in the Cotton Bowl; the first jet passenger trip had been taken; Dick Button had won his sixth U. S. skating title; and Julius and Ethel Rosenberg had been convicted of espionage.

Locally, the old Knoxville High School, the biggest rival of Fountain City's nearby Central High Bobcats, was preparing to graduate its final class. Four new high schools – Fulton, East, South, and West were nearing completion for opening in the fall.

The Hankins may have known, read, or heard about all these things, but the most important and exciting day to day thing in their lives at the time was their home and fulfilling the American Dream.

Fred, who was 31 years of age at the time, and Mary, age 27, had grown up together in the Corryton community of Knox County some 12 miles away. Fred's father had worked as a carpenter and a grocery store owner before moving to Fountain City and opening Fountain City Furniture Company. Mary, who had a twin sister, Martha, was the daughter of J. H. Tabler and Mallie Waller. Her father was a farmer.

Fred Hankins

Both Fred and Mary had grown up in and were members of Graveston Baptist Church in Corryton, where they still attended, and Mary taught a Sunday School class. Both had graduated from Gibbs High School, Fred in 1936 and Mary in 1941. Neither had dated anyone else before they married in 1946. They had no children.

A rumor persisted in the neighborhood that Mrs. Hankins was pregnant at the time of her death, but there was no corroboration of the rumor. Mrs. Hankins, a tall, very attractive brunette, had worked as a secretary at Standard Knitting Mills after graduating from high school and had only left that job when they moved into the new house.

Following lunch that day, Fred, who had made arrangements to have some work done on his car, drove to Hensley Motor Service at 5230 North Broadway in Fountain City, only five minutes away and located across the street from his father's furniture business. Don Severance, a 17-year-old Central High School student who worked after school and on Saturdays at Hensley's, drove Fred back to his home and returned to Hensley's with the Hankins' car.

After the work had been completed, Severance returned to the Hankins home around three o'clock with the car, picked up Fred, and they returned to the garage. Fred paid his bill and then went across the street and visited with his father for the better part of the next hour and a half.

Don Severance 1951

When Fred Hankins arrived back at the new Harrill Hills home shortly before five o'clock that afternoon, he expected to find his wife in the kitchen busily preparing their supper. Instead, when he reached the top of the basement steps and opened the door, he found Mary lying on the floor in a pool of her own blood.

Within a couple of hours a badly mutilated .32 caliber slug would be removed from her head at St. Mary's Hospital four miles away. Fred had no way of knowing then that the man who shot his wife would never be brought to trial or that of all the suspects questioned, the best suspect was over three years away from being named.

This man, along with two other suspects, had ties to a .32 caliber pistol. One such handgun, a revolver, proved by the FBI to have been the murder weapon, was recovered three and one-half months later eight miles from the Hankins' basement steps.

Fred Hankins knew nothing of what lay ahead. All he knew was that his wife had been mortally wounded, that she was dying, and that his life had been changed forever.

When he found Mary, she was bleeding so profusely from the head wound that her blood pool was starting to run through the basement doorway onto the top step. Terrified, his first reaction was to run for help, and that's what he did. He ran next door to the home of his neighbor, C. L. Holt, and yelled, "My wife's lying in a pool of blood! Come quick!"

Mr. Holt ran inside his house and called an ambulance and the Knox County Sheriff's Office while Mrs. Holt ran to the Hankins home with Mr. Hankins. When she saw Mary lying on the floor in the hallway between the kitchen and the basement door, she couldn't help but scream.

It wasn't long before an ambulance, other neighbors, sheriff's officers, and newspaper reporters descended on the scene. In fact, so many people contaminated the crime scene that officers concluded there was no point in processing the scene for latent fingerprints.

Fred was so distraught that he was barely able to relate the events of the day leading up to his returning home and finding his wife shot in the head. Mrs. Hankins died 30 minutes after arriving at St. Mary's Hospital. She never regained consciousness.

Amazingly, canvass of the neighborhood by sheriff's officers failed to locate anyone who heard a shot, and only one neighbor, Mrs. Jess E. (Mary Elizabeth) Schumaker, who lived diagonally across the road from the Hankins on the other corner of Forest and Crestwood, who had seen anyone other than the Hankins at their home.

A short time after Fred had left with the Severance teenager around 3:00 p.m., Mrs. Schumaker was out working in her front yard when she observed what she described as a black 1950 Ford bearing Knox County tags pull up in front of the Hankins home and park near the mailbox. (In 1951 two license plates were issued for display on both the front and the rear of the vehicle.)

Mrs. Schumaker noticed that the driver looked at the mailbox as he was getting out of the car. He was a "tall, lanky, slightly stooped man" but, being "a clothes conscious person," she took greater note of his dress than his physical characteristics. He was wearing a powder blue summer suit and a brown hat. Mrs. Schumaker recalled thinking to herself that he was not adequately dressed for the coolness of the day, pointing out that even though she was working and moving about, she had on three sweaters to keep warm.

Mary Elizabeth Schumaker

The unknown caller walked up to the front door and knocked rather loudly. When no one answered right away, he peeked in the small door window and then through the picture window to see if anyone was coming. Momentarily, Mrs. Hankins answered the door, and after only brief conversation, allowed him to enter and then closed the door.

Mrs. Schumaker would later say "you couldn't have counted to twelve before the man entered the house after he knocked." Additionally, friends and relatives would later describe Mrs. Hankins as the last person to allow a strange man to enter her home. She reportedly had just a few days before denied entry to a Fountain City minister until she was able to establish his identity.

After twenty minutes or so Mrs. Schumaker observed the man leaving and walking much more briskly than he had entered. He got in the black Ford and sped around the corner and past the front of her house. She was leaning over in the yard facing her house and only looked back between her body and her arm as he passed by. She never got a good look at him, later telling officers she could not identify him if she saw him again. She took no notice of anyone else in the car.

Knox County Coroner Sidney Wolfenbarger, upon examination of the crime scene and Mrs. Hankins, theorized she was shot while lying down. There were no powder burns found on her hair or scalp. The bullet entered the back top left of her head and lodged behind her right eye. Wolfenbarger opined that she was attempting to escape her attacker through the basement door when she was knocked to the floor and shot. A dish cloth found on or in front of the living room sofa led Wolfenbarger and others to believe that she and her assailant had sat on the sofa for a few minutes. There was no evidence of sexual assault.

The lead for the investigation was taken by Sheriff Clarence Walter "Buddy" Jones and his Chief Deputy, Paul H. Lilly. Jones, elected to office in August, 1950, would serve only one two-year term, 1950 – 1952. Lilly would win election to the sheriff's office in the 1956 race, but like Jones, would serve only one term.

Jones maintained a positive attitude about solving the murder but acknowledged from the outset that there were no hot leads to pursue. Chief Lilly was quoted as saying, "There are no motives. It's a most baffling murder."

Nothing was found missing from the house, and nothing was out of place other than the dish cloth found in the living room. The day after the murder of Mrs. Hankins, Sheriff Jones personally offered a $100 reward for information leading to the identity of the murderer and encouraged others to contribute toward the reward.

Mary Elizabeth Tabler Hankins was buried on Monday, two days after her murder, in the Graveston Cemetery in the Corryton community. Literally hundreds of grief-stricken relatives and friends attended the funeral at Graveston Baptist Church, the church Mary Hankins had attended all her life. There also were the curious, "the lookers," among those in attendance.

So many people attended that they overflowed into the rain swept churchyard. In anticipation of the numbers that would attend an outside speaker had been installed so everyone could hear the service.

Many of those among the throng in attendance had worked with Mrs. Hankins at Standard Knitting Mills, some for the entire decade she worked there. These same co-workers would call the sheriff's office daily for several days following the funeral in hopes of learning of new developments. Sadly, these friends never heard what they wanted to hear. Also attending the Hankins funeral were Sheriff Jones and six of his detectives.

Wedding Day 1946
Paul, Fred's Brother, Fred, Mary,
Martha, Mary's Twin Sister

Mary in Her 20's, 1944-1947

CHAPTER 2

DETACHED, INDEPENDENT INVESTIGATION

Two or three days following the murder, Fred Hankins reported that his wife's wrist watch was, in fact, missing. Unfortunately, the description of the watch was not circulated to pawn shops and other law enforcement agencies until August, almost five months after the murder.

According to an article that appeared in the August 24, 1951 issue of *The Knoxville News-Sentinel,* Assistant Attorney General Hal H. Clements, Jr. turned the information concerning the watch over to the City of Knoxville Record Bureau to prepare circulars for dissemination. Following is what the circulars related: "Attention pawn shops and police burglary detachments. Look out for a lady's yellow gold wrist watch, Gruen make, Model 21; movement, 2-753785; case No. 5922-363. Jewelry repair identifications on inside bottom of case: J-G-4-9-4."

Anyone with information was asked to contact Knoxville Chief of Police Joe Kimsey or Mr. Clements. Sheriff Jones' name, as well as Chief Lilly's name, were omitted from the circulars.

The Gruen 21 wristwatch was the first Gruen watch produced in the United States rather than Switzerland. This model watch was so named because it had a 21 jewel movement. It was produced in both round and rectangular 14k gold and gold-filled cases for both men and women. Production of the model 21 began in 1949 in the Cincinnati suburb of Norwood. The watch taken from Mrs. Hankins' wrist was, therefore, relatively new and would have been easily identifiable. The readily available detailed description furnished by Mr. Hankins suggests that Mrs. Hankins' Gruen watch was in all probability a birthday, Christmas, or anniversary gift from her husband.

The article concerning the watch circular also recounted the reward contributions begun by Sheriff Jones with $100. It listed contributors that included E. G. Tabler (victim's half-brother); Mrs. Mallie Tabler (victim's mother); George (Mayor of Knoxville), John, Bob, and Tom Dempster of Dempster Brothers, Incorporated; The News-Sentinel; Hite Sanford of East Tennessee Bonding Company; Bill Holland, a contractor; City Councilman Cas Walker; and two anonymous donors. The reward contributions at that time totaled $2,000.

Aside from publicizing a description of a critical piece of evidence in the case and listing the reward's contributors, this article drew attention to an extremely important aspect of this case and its investigation. The non-dissemination of the watch's description in a timely manner made it obvious that a critical piece of information had fallen through the cracks and that fingers were being pointed by Mr. Clements and Chief Kimsey at Sheriff Jones and Chief Lilly as those responsible for this oversight.

It was an oversight and a critical one. Almost five months had passed before this information was forwarded to people who might have either seen or received information about the evidentiary item. Any information developed about this watch shortly following the murder could have gone a long way in solving it.

Another aspect of the initial investigation that points to a lack of cooperation between county and city departments and borders on outright incompetence was the decision not to process the crime scene for latent fingerprints regardless of how many people may have contaminated the scene.

At some point, control could have been taken of the Hankins house in an effort to develop physical evidence, in particular, latent fingerprints. Mrs. Schumaker, being the clothes conscious person that she was, would certainly have noticed had the intruder been wearing gloves. She saw the intruder leave through the front door of the Hankins house, which meant that he touched the door knob, both inside and outside.

Criminalistics in 1951 were not what they are today, but there were people around who were trained in lifting and preserving latent fingerprints. The Knoxville Police Department had a section headed by a lieutenant with several examiners under his command who were trained and deemed competent. But someone had to request their assistance before they would have responded to a crime scene outside their jurisdiction.

Such a request was made of these examiners on September 20, 1949 by Sevier County Sheriff J. Roy Whaley after the brutally slain bodies of Charlie Perry and his live-in housekeeper were found at Perry's tourist court between Pigeon Forge and Gatlinburg. The Knoxville Police Department also furnished two detectives to assist and who, in fact, detained a Knoxville felon the following day as a suspect, a suspect whose name, in time, would surface in the Hankins case. The Perry case was solved as a result of the cooperation Sheriff Whaley received from neighboring Cocke County Sheriff Charles Fisher.

This spirit of cooperation did not exist between the Knox County Sheriff's Office and the Knoxville Police Department. No latent fingerprints were lifted at the crime scene or was any information ever developed concerning the watch. The lack of cooperation would not end here. Self-imposed department isolation by both departments would also affect future leads in the case.

CHAPTER 3

THE FIRST SUSPECTS

The first suspect jailed in connection with the Hankins murder was never publicly identified. He was picked up the day after the slaying and kept in custody for two nights. He was detained based on his physical description and his dress. He was wearing a light blue suit and a brown hat and apparently had been seen in the Fountain City area. Following two days of interrogation and a check of his alibi, he was released without ever being charged.

Another suspect later identified as Mrs. Hankins' cousin, W. R.(Bill) Tabler, was initially questioned on early Sunday morning and released. He was taken into custody for questioning again on Tuesday evening, and after two days of questioning, and after Knoxville attorney Erby Jenkins threatened to file a habeas corpus writ* to gain his release, he was released once again. Erby Jenkins was the law partner of, but no relation to, Ray Jenkins, who represented more murderers in East Tennessee than any other defense attorney of that era. The writ was never filed and Sheriff Jones agreed to voluntarily release him.

*A habeas corpus writ is a legal action through which a person can seek relief from unlawful detention, or the relief of another person, and thus protects persons from being harmed by the judicial system. The Latin definition is "You (shall) have the body." Such action was usually brought once a suspect had been detained beyond the 24-hour detention limit without being formally charged.

Jones was quoted in *The News-Sentinel* as saying, "I have nothing to hold him on. I have questioned him since Tuesday. He is from a respectable family and I don't want to embarrass him. I have nothing on this man up to now." According to a relative of the Tablers, Bill Tabler was considered a suspect because he had recently attempted to borrow some money from Mrs. Hankins and was upset because she refused to lend him the money.

Five months later, on the evening of August 30th, Tabler was arrested by a Knoxville police officer on North Broadway for drunken driving and carrying a pistol. At the time of his arrest a .32 caliber automatic wrapped in a bag was found lying on the car seat. Subsequent investigation by Sheriff Jones determined this German-made automatic was owned by a Donald C. Ross, a clerk in a West Depot Avenue tavern. Ross had bought the gun a week or so before and loaned it to Tabler to test fire.

Sheriff Jones was confident this was not the murder weapon as he knew the slug that killed Mrs. Hankins was fired from a revolver, not an automatic. Sheriff Jones explained, "I have an FBI report which shows that the murder weapon was a Colt revolver and not an automatic. Furthermore, an automatic requires a jacketed bullet, and the bullet found in the Hankins slaying was lead-coated. I am certain I already have the murder weapon." (The revolver referred to in the FBI report by Sheriff Jones had been recovered two months previously as detailed in Chapter 4.)

There were those who thought that Mary Hankins' family was somehow involved. These suspicions were fueled by articles in *The Knoxville Journal* during the days immediately following the murder suggesting disagreements among the Tablers as a result of the settlement of Mr. Tabler's estate.

Mary Hankins' mother was Mr. Tabler's second wife. He had grown children when his first wife died, and he remarried. The Tabler family was like two families within one.

Such speculation was invented because there was no apparent motive for this senseless killing, and these stories were being generated in an attempt to create a motive rather than find one. There was no credible evidence that pointed an accusing finger at anyone in the family.

And, of course, there were suspicions voiced, mostly in private, that Fred Hankins had paid someone to murder his wife. Those who knew Fred Hankins – the friends and relatives in the Corryton community and in Fountain City – knew that this possibility was less likely than one of the half-siblings or cousins having committed the murder.

Fred Hankins would move in with his parents following the murder and shortly thereafter put the new home at the corner of Forest Lane and Crestwood Road up for sale. Fred Hankins was a sad, broken man, not a murderer.

In time his wound would heal, and he would fill the void again with another twin from the Corryton community. In November, 1960, Mr. Hankins married Retha Dalton. They would share their love of golf together both in Knoxville and in the Florida sun at West Palm Beach where they wintered following their retirement. He would live out his remaining life of 39 years with this new love in Fountain City and die two days short of his 80th birthday.

Almost two years would pass before a legitimate suspect would be identified. There were rumors and reports of rumors but nothing solid materialized until February, 1953. Rumors of all kinds were particularly prevalent immediately following the murder.

Two weeks after Mrs. Hankins was slain, a north Knoxville businessman committed suicide in a Fountain City cemetery due to ill health, but before the facts were known, a rumor started that he killed himself because he was the Hankins murderer and his conscience had gotten the better of him. Shortly before this suicide the north Knoxville community had received another scare when a Fountain City housewife a mile away from the Hankins residence dropped a pistol and accidentally wounded herself in the chest.

In late August, 1951 *The News-Sentinel* reported that a private investigator had been hired by unidentified sources to solve the Hankins case. He was identified by the paper as H. B. Mayer, "free-lance detective, crime-story writer and erstwhile newspaper man and Army officer." Mayer, who preferred being addressed as "Colonel Mayer," declined to disclose his reason for being in Knoxville to *The News-Sentinel.*

Mayer reportedly had come to Knoxville from Gulfport, Mississippi where he had been investigating the slayings of Knoxvillians Helen Armetta Stewart and her 6-year-old son. The brutally beaten bodies of Mrs. Stewart, a 29-year-old divorcee, and her son, Howard, had been found floating in the surf just west of Gulfport on May 27th. Mrs. Stewart had been so brutally beaten that her sister, Cecelia Armetta, also of Knoxville, identified her sister by a mole on an ear and a birthmark on a foot. The boy had been beaten so badly in the back of the head that the Gulfport sheriff was quoted as saying, "it looked like an egg shell."

There were no similarities between the Stewart and Hankins cases. A 64-year-old eccentric recluse from Picayune, Mississippi was developed as a suspect in the Stewart murders four days later after a child's sleeping garment and a burlap sack bearing what appeared to be blood was found in the hermit's truck. Colonel Mayer had also hosted a radio series on the case while in Gulfport.

Sheriff Jones, when asked about the reported hiring of a private investigator, responded, "I've learned that a special investigator has been hired privately to solve the Hankins case. I'd be only too pleased to see it solved by any one at all. I don't care how the case is solved, so long as it is solved. We're continuing to bend every effort to clean up this case. There have been some developments, but it wouldn't be in the interest of a solution to divulge all of them."

The News-Sentinel also contacted Attorney General Clements and asked if his office had any arrangement with the private investigator. Clements said he knew nothing about it.

As for Colonel Mayer, whether hired by someone or free-lancing on his own, he was attempting to develop leads and information for publication in one of the popular detective magazines of that time. Nothing was ever published, however, as Mayer ran into the same wall that Sheriff Jones and his detectives had been bucking up against for five months. Colonel Mayer left town without solving the murder or developing a viable suspect.

The publishers of the detective magazines that were so prevalent at the time of the Hankins murder wanted sensationalized accounts of gruesome solved murders with photographs of victims, charged suspects, and law enforcement officers responsible for solving the cases. The Hankins case offered none of these.

The typical cover of these magazines depicted a sexy, voluptuous female crime victim striking a seductive pose on a bed. These magazines were hideous mixes of embellished crime accounts and "girly magazines." Shock and sensationalism sold these monthly offerings, not facts.

The 1950 Roane County murder of Robert Grant for which Leon Luallen and two other defendants were convicted satisfied the requirements of the detective magazine publishers. An account of that case appeared in the July, 1950 issue of *Inside Detective* and was titled "Bellyfull of Murder."

Following is the cover of the April, 1950 issue of *Timely Detective* which magazine contained, among other things, an account of the Perry's Camp murders in Sevier County in September, 1949. The second cover is that of the July, 1950 issue of *Inside Detective* which carried an account of the Robert Grant murder in Roane County.

Timely Detective, **April 1950**

Inside Detective, **July 1950**

CHAPTER 4

RECOVERY OF THE MURDER WEAPON

During the early 1950s a favorite Knox County car-washing spot, especially for residents of North Knox County, was a small, unnamed creek that flowed along the west side of Norris Freeway (U. S. Highway 441) into Bull Run Creek. It was for that reason that John C. Johnson, a retired farmer living on Jacksboro Road, accompanied by his son, Jack, went to that location on Sunday afternoon, June 17th, two and one-half months after the Hankins murder.

The spot they normally used was crowded with picnickers, so they moved a bit downstream from their usual place. The younger Johnson went first to the creek to get a bucket of water and returned with the bucket only half full. Disgusted, the father then went to the creek to get a full bucket. To do so, however, he had to push through the bushes to a deeper spot in the stream. It was then that he caught a glimmer of the pearl-handled pistol in about six inches of water.

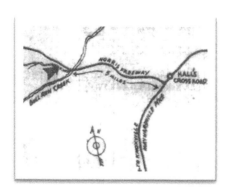

(Heavy black arrow shows gun location.)

Johnson called his son over, and after retrieving the gun and examining it, they both concluded that this could be the murder weapon in the Hankins murder. They determined it was a .32 caliber Colt revolver. It had one spent cartridge in the cylinder. The other five cartridges were still intact. The spot where they had found the gun was eight miles from the Hankins' home.

Ironically, a search had been made of another body of water for the murder weapon just days after the murder. The Fountain City "duck pond" on North Broadway at Cedar Lane had been drained of several thousand gallons of water but no gun was found. This time, purely by chance, a gun was found in water that had real potential of being the murder weapon.

After realizing what they may have found, the Johnsons wiped the gun off, wrapped it up and headed for town. They drove to the Knox County Sheriff's Office and talked to Chief Jailer Pete Jones. Jones, who immediately reached the same conclusion as the Johnsons, took the Johnsons to Sheriff Jones' house out in Fountain City.

Sheriff Jones was convinced that the Johnsons had found the murder weapon. He swore both of them to secrecy and did not make their identities known until three weeks later.

The picture that follows depicts Johnson reading about his discovery of the gun in the July 14, 1951 issue of *The Knoxville News-Sentinel.*

John C. Johnson

The following morning Sheriff Jones boarded a flight to Washington and personally took the suspected murder weapon, still loaded with cartridges as found, and the slug removed from Mrs. Hankins' head, to the FBI Laboratory for examination. He called ahead to make arrangements for the gun to be examined immediately, which it was.

Sheriff Jones had known from the outset that the recovered slug was too mutilated for ballistic analysis, and he was not certain what the laboratory might be able to determine with what he now had. The FBI Laboratory was soon able to tell him that the .32 caliber slug removed from the victim had been molded on the same Winchester Arms Company machine which molded the five un-fired bullets found in the Colt's cylinder.

Even more remarkable, the laboratory concluded that the fingerprints on the cartridges were there when the gun was thrown into the creek, and that the water had served as a chemical agent to further etch the prints into the brass cartridge cases. At first Sheriff Jones was under the impression the fingerprints were probably those of someone who handled the gun after it was removed from the water, that is, the Johnsons, his officers, or himself. He was assured by the FBI Laboratory that the prints were there when the gun went into the creek and "said it was one of the most extraordinary findings they'd ever come across."

Colt Revolver with Slug and Cartridges

During the ensuing weeks Sheriff Jones began the laborious task of trying to trace the origin of this blue-steel 6-shot Colt revolver with a 4 ½ inch barrel and pearl handles, Serial No. 112423. Beginning on July 11th, both daily Knoxville papers, *The Journal* and *The News-Sentinel,* ran photographs of the gun and its description and thereafter reported everything learned about the gun by Sheriff Jones and the papers' own reporters.

Sheriff Jones acknowledged at that time that he had almost given up until this unexpected break. He had accumulated the fingerprints of more than 100 persons of anyone considered possibly even remotely connected to the murder, but now he had the murder weapon and the probable owner's prints. Jones was quoted as saying, "I've made plane trips to Birmingham and Florida and New York on this case, and was about to fly to a foreign country once – all turned out to be blind leads." Sheriff Jones was obviously encouraged and enthused by the discovery of this Colt revolver.

The tracing of this handgun proved to be very difficult and not very productive. The investigation pretty quickly determined through Colt Arms Company that the gun was originally sold in January 1914 to C. M. McClung Company, a large hardware wholesaler in Knoxville. C. M. McClung in turn sold two .32 caliber Colt revolvers, one blue-steel and one nickel-plated, to a Reliable Trading Company on June 30, 1914.

Reliable Trading Company was subsequently determined to have operated at Kodak, Tennessee in Sevier County between 1913 and 1916. The owners of this business were then identified, and one of them, a Luther Q. Bailey of Rockford still had an old ledger from Reliable Trading but found no information concerning the sale of the gun. In fact, Bailey had no recollection of the company ever having sold a gun of any description. Bailey recalled, "The only gun we ever had in the store was one shotgun we sold off a punch board."

Sheriff Jones was, even in view of the lack of records from Reliable Trading Company, able to determine that two revolvers were purchased from Reliable Trading Company in 1914. An unidentified citizen had contacted the sheriff and advised him that his father had purchased a .32 caliber revolver from Reliable Trading Company in 1914 at the same time that a Hugh L. White had purchased a .32 caliber revolver. The source advised Sheriff Jones that his father's revolver was nickel-plated, but that he did not know what the finish was on the revolver purchased by White.

Sheriff Jones was able to develop only one lead on a Hugh L. White. This man was a former resident of Tazewell who had moved to North Vernon, Indiana, some 50 miles north of Louisville, Kentucky. This man's son, Ralph White, a Knoxville resident, advised his father was only nine years of age in 1914. Sheriff Jones and Chief Lilly continued their efforts to locate a Hugh L. White who might have purchased the gun in question from Reliable Trading Company in 1914, but no other person by this name was ever located. The owners of this revolver were not determined during Jones' term in office.

Had Ancestry.com been available to Sheriff Jones in 1951 he could have determined that a Hugh L. White, age 45 in 1914, and born in Hawkins County, lived at Whitesburg in Hamblen County and that his father, William White, had furnished his occupation in the 1880 U. S. Census as a "farmer and distiller." It would have been reasonable in 1914 for someone from Hamblen County buying a gun from C. M. McClung to have ordered through a company in Kodak, which was located between Whitesburg and Knoxville.

Another lead that was being investigated during the time this revolver was being traced had to do with a magazine salesman reported to have been in the Harrill Hills area the day of the murder. The salesman maintained he was in Harriman in Roane County that day, not Knox County. Chief Lilly was quoted as saying, "We checked on him and two other magazine salesmen. Their alibis seem to stand up. However, we have sent their fingerprints to Washington for a further check."

The FBI's Comparison of Recovered Slug with Unspent Cartridges

The comparative bullet-lead analysis (CBLA), also known as compositional bullet-lead analysis, according to most all accounts, was first used by the FBI Laboratory during the early 1960s. In fact, it reportedly was first used to analyze the mutilated slugs recovered in the assassination of President Kennedy in 1963.

CBLA was used in those instances where the recovered slug(s) were too mutilated to allow for a ballistics comparison. The theory was that each batch of ammunition possessed a unique elemental or chemical make-up and could be traced back to a particular batch, or even a specific box.

Following internal FBI studies and an external study conducted by the National Academy of Sciences, the technique was found unreliable, and the FBI discontinued use of this analysis in 2005. The results of the analyses had been brought into question by defense attorneys and the media. The methods of the FBI Laboratory concerning this analysis, which correlated trace elements such as arsenic, antimony, tin, copper, bismuth, silver and cadmium, were not questioned, but rather the ambiguity with which the results were related to law enforcement and thus to the courts. The opportunity for the defense to challenge the results were limited inasmuch as the FBI was the only crime laboratory that conducted such analyses, which precluded defense attorneys from presenting evidence from other "expert" witnesses.

The National Academy of Sciences did not question the FBI's techniques or procedures, pointing out that the confusion came about in communicating the results. The Academy did not require the FBI to discontinue CBLA, but in 2004, the FBI made the decision to voluntarily stop offering this analyses to law enforcement and discontinued the service the following year.

Opponents of CBLA have never been successful in efforts to force the U. S. government to release the estimated 2,500 cases in which the FBI performed CBLA which may have led to tainted convictions. According to the FBI only about 500 of these cases in which such analyses were performed actually resulted in the CBLA evidence being introduced at trial. As a result of the 2004 report, the murder conviction of a Florida inmate, obtained largely on the admission of bullet-lead analysis evidence, was overturned and the inmate was released.

Obviously, the Kennedy assassination was not the first time that the FBI laboratory used bullet-lead analysis to match a mutilated slug with other cartridges or batches of bullets. This analysis, or one very similar to the one used in the Kennedy case had been used in the Hankins case a dozen of years previously.

CHAPTER 5

THE UNDOING OF SHERIFF JONES

C. W. "Buddy" Jones was the first Democrat to be elected Sheriff of Knox County in 18 years when he was voted into office in 1950. He had the support of Democratic Governor Gordon Browning and Democratic Knoxville Mayor George Dempster. He defeated two-term Republican incumbent Austin Cate, whose father, William T. Cate, had been sheriff, and who had worked for the Knox County Sheriff's Department in some capacity for many years.

When the Hankins murder occurred in March, 1951 Jones' law enforcement experience was limited. Although a Knoxville businessman, he had been appointed warden at Brushy Mountain State Prison at Petros in 1949 when Warden Glenn Swafford was promoted to warden at the Tennessee State Penitentiary in Nashville. Jones resigned his post as warden at Brushy Mountain on March 1, 1950 reportedly to devote full time to his business interests in Knoxville, which included a boating business. Not unexpectedly, however, Jones entered the Democratic primary seeking his party's nomination for sheriff the next month.

Jones' stiffest competition for the Democratic nomination came from Charles Lobetti, a Knoxville Police Department detective with 15 years experience. Jones, with the support of the local and state Democratic organizations, defeated Lobetti and went on to defeat Cate in the general election four months later. Jones, a military firearms expert and marksman, a state skeet shooting champion, and a former representative for Remington Firearms Company, had made an unsuccessful bid for sheriff two years previously.

Interestingly, the April 22, 1950 Democratic Primary ballot included four former University of Tennessee football players. William W. Luttrell, a tackle in the late 1930's, was seeking re-election to his post as Finance Commissioner. Charles W. (Pug) Vaughn, a tailback in the mid-1930's, was seeking nomination for welfare commissioner; Robert L. (Bob) Suffridge, an All-American guard in the late 1930's, was seeking the office of county clerk; and J. Fred Moses, a tailback in the mid-1930's, was seeking nomination for county solicitor.

During Jones' tenure at Brushy Mountain, he handled two well-known and widely publicized situations. The first, which took place on June 30, 1949, involved two guards at the prison. The two men, known to be "best friends," became embroiled in an argument over labor unions. The argument ended with both men shooting one another, one suffering fatal wounds. The surviving guard was never charged.

The second incident, which occurred on February 1, 1950, was a massive landslide which, according to Jones, brought down "thousands and thousands of tons of mud and slime" from Frozenhead Mountain down onto the prison enclosure. For 15 hours, the slide blocked the highway and rail line into the prison as well as two of the three coal mines on the mountain's face. The slide was removed with the use of a bulldozer and inmate labor.

A couple of months after Jones was elected Knox County Sheriff, he would announce the arrest of Ed Roddy, 58, in the pistol slaying of his neighbor, 38-year-old Edgar M. Ferguson. Ferguson had been missing for 10 days when Roddy admitted to the murder and informed sheriff detectives of the location of Ferguson's body. It would be five months before C. Fred Hankins would return to his Fountain City home to find his wife dying of a gunshot wound that would prove to be the most baffling crime of Jones' term in office, and his greatest nemesis.

Regrettably for Sheriff Jones, he had been quoted at the outset of the Hankins murder investigation as saying, "I'm not going to bed until we crack this case." Jones would leave office after serving one term without having made an arrest in the Hankins case and would bear the nickname "Sleepless" Jones for the rest of his life.

While the details of Mrs. Hankins' slaying would fade and become unclear, Sheriff Jones' nickname would always be remembered and associated with the case. To this day, mention of this tragedy to most who were living at the time immediately brings to mind "Sleepless" Jones rather than the circumstances surrounding her death.

"Sleepless" Jones

Sheriff Jones wanted very badly to solve the Hankins murder while still in office. He made the statement that earned him an unwanted nickname to emphasize his fervent desire to find her killer. He started a reward fund with a personal contribution of $100 and encouraged others to follow his lead, which they did. Even after being defeated for re-election by Sheriff Cate, he was an interested by-stander when Joseph Hegler, and later, Bill Luallen, became suspects. Even in view of all this, the word most frequently used to described Sheriff Jones' legacy would not be "crime-solver," but rather, "Sleepless."

CHAPTER 6

THE HEGLER AFFAIR

**"Heaven has no rage like love to hatred turned,
nor hell a fury like a woman scorned."**
-Congreve, *Mourning Bride,* 1697

In December, 1952 Knoxville Police Chief Joe Kimsey and Knox County Sheriff Austin Cate, "Sleepless" Jones' successor, would each receive basically the same information concerning the Hankins killing from two different sources, but which originated from the same source. The men shared little of the information until it became public two months later. Each launched their own independent investigation.

Sheriff Cate's department had primary jurisdiction in the case as the murder of Mrs. Hankins had occurred in Knox County, not within the Knoxville city limits, and was under no obligation to share its information. Chief Kimsey's obligation appears to have been held in check for political reasons. He conducted his investigation in secret at the behest of his boss, Mayor Dempster, who had supported Sheriff Jones for re-election, not Cate, during the previous year's election.

Based on the information he had received, Chief Kimsey swore out two arrest warrants for one Joseph Buick Hegler before two different city judges on Tuesday and Wednesday, February 10 and 11, 1953. City Judge Charles G. Kelly signed one of the arrest warrants, but fearing that it might not be sufficient, Kimsey obtained a second arrest warrant signed by Sessions Court Judge Alfred Frazier. Both judges were sworn to secrecy.

Chief Kimsey had been in contact with police authorities in Aiken, South Carolina, who had arrested Hegler and were holding him for Kimsey to arrive and take him into custody. On Friday, armed with the arrest warrants, Kimsey boarded a private plane at Island Home Airport for Aiken, where he took custody of Hegler, who had already waived extradition, and returned to Knoxville with him the same day. Kimsey was flown to South Carolina by Tom Kesterson, a well-known Knoxville aviator who operated a charter flying service out of Island Home Airport.

Before Chief Kimsey touched down at Island Home that afternoon, Mayor Dempster had already announced the arrest to the Knoxville newspapers and related the evidence that had been developed by Chief Kimsey. Mayor Dempster it seemed, not only wanted to upstage Sheriff Cate, but also wanted to be the first to broadcast the news that this puzzling homicide that had baffled Knoxville lawmen for almost two years was finally going to be solved. And … was going to be solved by the Knoxville Police Department.

Mayor Dempster went so far as to order Chief Kimsey to bring Hegler by the mayor's office before doing anything else with him. Dempster identified Jessie Waldroup, a divorcee and waitress who lived at 833 North Third Avenue, as having furnished a statement to Chief Kimsey accusing Hegler of Mrs. Hankins' murder.

Mrs. Waldroup, age 31, who was working at the Cameron Restaurant at 639 Broadway a few blocks from her North Third Avenue apartment, identified Hegler, age 36, as a former boyfriend with whom she had lived in Knoxville and Detroit, and the father of her youngest child. They had separated after having "a falling out," but she was repeatedly described as a "jilted lover" and a "woman scorned" in the Knoxville papers.

Mrs. Waldroup alleged that she was with Hegler when he was selling magazines and was in the car when he drove to the Hankins' home on the afternoon of the murder. Hegler stopped in front of the house, got out and went to the door and was let in by Mrs. Hankins. After a few minutes he came hurriedly back to the car and when she asked him what had happened, she quoted him as saying, "I just had to kill a woman. I'll blow your head off if you don't keep your mouth shut."

When later asked how she explained the fact that a witness never saw her in the car, she explained that she was crouched down in the front seat reading a newspaper.

By the time Hegler was arrested and brought to Knoxville and placed in the Knoxville city jail before being transferred to the Knox County jail, Mrs. Waldroup had already been questioned several times by both Chief Kimsey and Sheriff Cate. She had not come forward willingly and had been reluctant to give a statement to anyone.

Chief Kimsey had learned from an unnamed associate of Waldroup that she may have some information about the Hankins murder. Cate learned of Waldroup as a result of a referral from the local FBI office. A source informed the FBI that Waldroup possessed information concerning the killing, and this information was passed along to the Knox County Sheriff's Office.

Kimsey and Cate of course learned of each other's investigation and had agreed not to make an arrest without the other. Kimsey had received instructions to handle the matter differently and had been unable to contact Cate before Dempster broke the case to the media.

All this secrecy, trickery, and deceit made for a strained joint investigation and as the ensuing week wore on, the majority of the investigation, i. e., interviewing Waldroup and Hegler and checking Hegler's alibi, was conducted by Knox County authorities rather than the City of Knoxville. Chief Kimsey's jumping the gun and arresting Hegler prematurely, even though brought on by pressure from his boss, was extremely unfortunate. Had a proper joint investigation been conducted, it would have revealed Hegler's alibi, which as it turned out, was a good one.

Hegler had from the outset not only denied the murder, but had denied all the allegations made by his former paramour. He denied he was even in Knoxville on the day of the murder but rather was working on a job with E. I. du Pont in the Pisgah National Forest near Asheville, North Carolina. He insisted he had never sold magazines. At the time of his arrest in South Carolina Hegler was working as a boom painter on an "H-bomb project."

Hegler initially denied ever having been arrested for anything other than drunken driving for which he was not convicted. Hegler also subsequently admitted to a juvenile larceny charge in Tampa, Florida after being confronted by Knox County detectives with evidence of this charge.

During the course of interviewing Mrs. Waldroup, she was asked about any guns Hegler may have had in his possession, and responded that she had given Hegler a .25 caliber handgun that she had bought from a bail bondsman. When shown the .32 caliber Colt revolver recovered from the creek just off Norris Freeway, she said it appeared similar to a gun Hegler had in his possession a week before the murder.

Jessie Waldrop & Joseph B. Hegler

During the week Hegler was in custody both he and Mrs. Waldroup were interviewed several times in rooms only feet apart. There were times that Hegler became so upset and emotional that he broke down and cried. On the third day they had the occasion to confront one another for the first time, and each of them repeatedly told the other that they were lying. Both steadfastly stuck to their stories.

On Monday, the same day Hegler and Waldroup confronted one another, Hegler's newly-retained attorneys, Ray H. Jenkins and Erby L. Jenkins, filed a habeas corpus writ in Criminal Court seeking Hegler's release. The hearing was set for the following afternoon. Hegler's attorneys had been hired the previous day by Hegler's brother, Charles J. Hegler, of Tampa.

Ray Jenkins had represented multiple murder defendants and had the reputation of being the best defense attorney in East Tennessee. Erby Jenkins had already represented one suspect in the Hankins case – W. R. (Bill) Tabler – and had gained his release by the mere threat of filing a habeas corpus writ. This time, however, the decision

41

as to whether Hegler should remain in custody or be released would be made in a court room. That decision, whether made by a judge or Knox County's District Attorney General, Hal H. Clements, Jr., hinged on whether Hegler's alibi could be disputed or verified.

For the week Hegler had been in custody, a substantial amount of effort had been expended by Sheriff Cate, his detectives, Chief Kimsey, and General Clements in an attempt to answer the all-important question: Was Hegler working on Saturday, March 31, 1951 in the Pisgah National Forest in Western North Carolina, at least three and one-half hours away, or was he in Knoxville as alleged by his former girlfriend and mother of one of his six children?

The culmination of this drama had reached a fever pitch by the time Criminal Court Judge J. Fred Bibb banged his gavel at 1:00 p.m. on Tuesday, February 17th. The courtroom was packed to the point that there were people standing around the sides and rear of the room. Spectators were even sitting in the jury box. Had the jury box been empty and an out-of-towner had mistakenly wandered in the stranger almost certainly would have thought a jury verdict was waiting to be heard.

The payroll records of E. I. du Pont had finally arrived from Wilmington, Delaware after extensive searching by a whole bevy of corporate workers. Hegler's time card showed that he clocked in at work the day of the murder at 7:42 a. m. and clocked out at 4:33 p. m.

In addition, there were two corroborating witnesses waiting in the wings to testify if needed. Mack C. Davis, the painters union business agent on the Pisgah job, was ready to testify that he and Hegler had discussed union wage negotiations in the company office on the day in question. Davis also contended that it would have been impossible for another worker to have clocked Hegler in and out that day as there was always a guard on duty at the time clock.

Another co-worker, Hugh Clark, was prepared to testify that he and Hegler had ridden to work together every day and had only missed one Saturday, this being in November, 1950 due to a snow storm. The Pisgah job was a six-day work week, and Saturdays were significant because those were overtime days.

At the beginning of the hearing, City Law Director Clarence Blackburn advised Judge Bibb that Chief Kimsey was in North Carolina "working on the case" and requested the hearing be postponed until Kimsey returned. General Clements responded by saying he didn't think that a postponement would be fair to Hegler in view of the extensive investigation already conducted.

Clements recommended that the petition (habeas corpus writ) be sustained and Blackburn said the city would accept the Attorney General's recommendation. Judge Bibb said, "regardless of the city's request, the opinion of the attorney general governs the court." noting that "General Clements represents us all."

Clements related to Judge Bibb and the packed courtroom that the evidence of Hegler's presence on a construction job near Asheville on the day of the slaying was "conclusive and overwhelming." Clements related the times Hegler had worked, making it "physically impossible" for him to have been in Knoxville at the time of the murder.

Judge Bibb advised that under a habeas corpus writ he could not decide the guilt or innocence of a person but must determine if the person is illegally held. Hegler's attorneys, Ray and Erby Jenkins, then agreed to dismiss the petition and Clements then advised Sheriff Cate to release Hegler, which he did.

When the sound of Judge Bibb's gavel marked the conclusion of the hearing, Hegler, clad in his now customary khaki work clothes, was mobbed by both women and men who could not hold back their emotions as he stood sobbing and red-faced. Afterwards Hegler told the press that "the greatest shock of my life came when I learned I had been charged with the heinous crime of murder. I had never even heard of Mrs. Hankins. I had no motive to murder." Hegler continued, "I naturally felt indignant that I was accused of the crime but in the conscience of my innocence waived extradition before I even left the H-bomb plant and voluntarily came to Knoxville to face this charge, believing in the justice of our courts and in the sense of decency and fair play of the people in Tennessee."

Hegler also commented that he felt his case was handled in reverse – that he was arrested first and then the investigation was conducted. He felt it should have been handled the other way around. Hegler was quoted as saying that the unwarranted charge of murder "has put a scar on me that will never be healed." He left the courthouse hoping that his job was still waiting for him in Aiken, South Carolina.

General Clements made other statements during the hearing which cast doubt on Chief Kimsey's investigation and premature arrest of Hegler. Clements stated that he and his county investigators were doubtful that Hegler was responsible for the Hankins murder from the outset of the investigation in spite of the accusations of Mrs. Waldroup.

Clements revealed that Mrs. Waldroup was unable to furnish sufficient details, pointing out she could not accurately describe the Hankins house, telling them the house was a white frame house when, in fact, it was brick. Neither did she have any recollection of dirt piled up around the recently-completed home the day the murder took place. Clements described the alibi evidence provided by Hegler's former employer in North Carolina as being better than if he had been in jail.

In the end, the "scorned woman" and "jilted lover" phrases used to describe Jessie Waldroup turned out to be the vindictive reasons behind her accusations. Hegler had left her after they had a child together for another woman. Hegler had that way about him and apparently considered himself a "lady's man." During the plane ride from Aiken to Knoxville he had told Chief Kimsey he had been married twice and had his eye on his third wife in South Carolina. He had a child by each of his wives but acknowledged having two or three children by women to whom he had not been married.

Mrs. Waldroup's contention that Hegler was selling magazines was believable inasmuch as this had played a part in the investigation of the Hankins murder when it occurred. Magazine salesmen who had been working in the Harrill Hills area had been located and questioned. In fact, it was determined that Mrs. Hankins had recently purchased a magazine subscription. All this had, however, been well publicized in 1951 and magazine salesmen were commonplace. In fact, door-to-door sales of a number of items were commonplace in the '50s – magazines, Bibles, Electro-Lux vacuum cleaners, and Fuller Brush products just to mention a few. Some doctors were still making house calls. Such marketing and medical practices are not unheard of today – except for doctors' house calls - but are much less prevalent.

Almost nine years after leaving the Knox County courtroom of Judge Bibb, Hegler would be in another courtroom, a Federal courtroom in Tampa. This time, however, he would be in this courtroom to testify as a witness, not to defend himself against uncorroborated charges.

Hegler was called to testify in a bank robbery conspiracy trial in U. S. District Court, Southern District of Florida, Tampa Division. One of the four defendants had entered a guilty plea prior to commencement of the trial and agreed to testify against the other defendants. Two of the remaining three were found guilty while the remaining defendant was found not guilty by virtue of a directed verdict for acquittal.

Hegler was called by the Government to corroborate the testimony of the cooperating defendant by furnishing identifying information concerning one of the other defendants. Obviously, Hegler knew the defendant but his testimony is no longer available. The cooperating defendant was the only person charged in this conspiracy found to be alive as of April 2010. He was contacted April 8, 2010 but recalled no details about Hegler, his testimony, or his relationship with the defendant.

Joseph Buick Hegler was residing at Swainsboro, Georgia at the time of his death at Milledgeville, Georgia in February 1993 at age 75.

Postscript

As was expected the political ramifications continued in this case after Hegler had left Knox County. A week to the day after Judge Bibb's courtroom was cleared, Knoxville City Councilman Cas Walker sponsored a resolution of apology to Hegler from the City of Knoxville.

Walker offered the resolution based on the grounds that Mayor Dempster had been directly responsible for the arrest and subsequent grilling of Hegler. Walker purported that the city was in danger of being sued unless it adopted such a resolution. Walker reminded the council of Hegler's "scarred for life" statement following the court hearing a week earlier.

Mayor Dempster refused to sign off on the resolution, saying "I ordered the arrest of this man … and sent the chief of police over there. He was brought to my office on my orders … It was not my intention to do an injustice to anybody." No action was taken by the council on the resolution, but Walker had made his point.

The citizens of Knoxville and Knox County would have been disappointed if the discord between Mayor Dempster and Councilman Walker had not been a part of this fiasco arrest of an innocent man. People had come to expect public jabs between these two very public Knoxville businessmen and politicians. George Dempster and Cas Walker had become bitter political enemies over the years.

Dempster, a Democrat, was born in Knoxville and grew up in an influential, affluent family while Walker, a Republican, "came up the hard way" in neighboring Sevier County. Both were self-made men with substantial political clout. Dempster and his brothers invented and manufactured the Dempster Dumpster used for the collection and disposal of waste. Walker established a chain of supermarkets in East

Tennessee that extended to Pennington Gap, Virginia, easily identified by "the sign of the shears." Dempster during the late '20s and early '30s lived in one of the most fashionable homes in Fountain City and in all likelihood knew the Hankins, in particular, J. E. Hankins, owner of Fountain City Furniture Company. Walker's home for years was in the North Hills area of Knoxville.

Dempster had served as Knoxville City Manager on three occasions before being elected to the City Council in 1947 and to the Mayor's office in 1951. He and Walker, who served on the City Council and as Mayor over a three-decade span, battled incessantly. The quote most often attributed to Dempster about Walker was, "If I ordered a boxcar load of sons of bitches and they only sent me Cas, I'd pay for the whole order."

George Dempster

Cas Walker, nicknamed "The Ole Coon Hunter," was an icon of East Tennessee mountain culture. During the '50s he sponsored a musical variety show and a gospel singing show on local television and pitched his groceries on both shows himself. The "Cas Walker Farm and Home Hour" helped launch the careers of the Everly Brothers and Dolly

Parton while "Mull's Singing Convention," hosted by J. Bazzel Mull, his neighbor, aired for decades.

Cas Walker

Some viewed Cas Walker as a champion for the common man while others saw him as an embarrassment. Walker frequently referred to Dempster's political supporters as "the silk stocking gang."

Walker's barb at Dempster over the Hegler affair would not be his last. The two men probably still had as many barbs left to swap that they had already exchanged in past years. Culturally and politically, they shared very little. Both men were strong-willed and threw hard punches. At the end of their lives they shared one commonality – they both died during the month of September. Dempster died in 1964 at age 77; Walker, in 1998 at age 96.

CHAPTER 7

THE BEST SUSPECT

**"Witnesses are like relatives;
you're born with them."**
-Unknown prosecutor(s)

James William "Bill" Luallen, born June 22, 1920, was one of ten children - six sons and four daughters - born to Delous Lafayette "Dallas" Luallen and Harriet Elizabeth Hunley, both of whom were born in Coal Creek in Anderson County, Tennessee. Coal Creek, which later became Lake City, was near the Fraterville Mine where a mine explosion in 1902 claimed 216 lives.

After Dallas served a stint in the U. S. Navy, the couple married in 1909 and moved to Knoxville where they raised their family. Harriett also had a son by a previous suitor. Dallas and Harriett Luallen divorced in 1944, but both continued to live in Knoxville.

Dallas Luallen took a job with Southern Railroad as a switchman. He worked for Southern for over 30 years. Two of his sons would in the early '50s be sentenced to prison for murder, and one, Daniel Leon Luallen, would spend most of his adult life in prison.

Bill Luallen, imprisoned for numerous theft charges since the early 1940s, would become a prime suspect in the murder of Mary Hankins during the same time frame his brothers were imprisoned for two separate killings. Bill Luallen would, like his brother, Leon, spend most of his life in prison, a large part of it at Brushy Mountain State Prison at Petros.

Brushy Mountain State Prison 1966

Bill Luallen began his criminal career in 1936 at the age of 15 when he was sent to the State Vocational Training School in Nashville for stealing a car. The following year he received his first sentence for housebreaking and larceny and was again confined to the Nashville reform school. His first incarceration as an adult was in 1939 when he was convicted of housebreaking and larceny in Knox County and was sentenced to six years.

In 1942 Luallen was sentenced to 3-4 years for the same offense and admitted to having broken into 32 houses, several located in prominent sections of Knoxville. He escaped from a work camp at Shelbyville on April 22, 1943 after being moved there from Brushy Mountain State Prison at Petros.

Luallen was on the lam for almost a year before being arrested for house burglary in Indianapolis (Marian County), Indiana. In April, 1944 Luallen received a sentence of 10-20 years for first degree burglary and was incarcerated at the Indiana State Penitentiary in Michigan City, Indiana.

Indiana State Penitentiary Circa 1930

On August 28, 1943, prior to Bill Luallen's arrest for burglary in Indianapolis, the body of Maoma L. Ridings, a 32-year-old WAC (Women's Army Corps) Corporal stationed at Camp Atterbury near Edinburgh, Indiana, was found slain in a guest room of the Claypool Hotel in Indianapolis. Corporal Ridings, divorced and a native of Warm Springs, Georgia, where she had at one time worked as a nurse for President Roosevelt, apparently had checked into the hotel for the weekend while on leave from nearby Camp Atterbury. Her body was found nude from the waist down, and her death had been caused by a blow to the head and lacerations on her throat and wrists inflicted with a broken whiskey bottle found near the body. Only 21 cents was found among her belongings.

Initially, a bell boy at the hotel who claimed to have served Ridings ice about two hours before her body was found was held as a suspect but was never charged. Another bell boy described "a woman in black" that he had seen in Ridings' room where they were having "a wild party" shortly before the slaying, but this woman was never identified and located. The case dragged on without any leads of substance. No arrest was made until October 1944, six months after Luallen was sentenced to 10-20 years for burglary.

On October 25, 1944 Wynona Luallen, the former wife of Bill Luallen, was arrested in Knoxville for the murder of Ridings based on a statement furnished by her ex-husband. In the statement, Luallen claimed his ex-wife had confessed the murder to him. She was also charged with participating with him in two daylight burglaries in Marian County, Indiana.

Mrs. Luallen unexpectedly waived extradition and agreed to return to Indianapolis for questioning. Mrs. Luallen, nee Yoe, and Bill Luallen had been married in 1940, but she divorced him in 1943. Mrs. Luallen, after being extradited to Indianapolis, repeatedly denied any involvement in the Ridings killing. She insisted her former husband was lying about the murder as well as his accusation that she assisted him in two Indianapolis burglaries.

Wynona Luallen & Bill Luallen in 1944

Six days later, Bill Luallen, also known to Indiana authorities as William Larry Luallen, recanted his accusations against Wynona and confessed to the slaying of Ridings himself. In a signed statement Luallen alleged to have killed Ridings with a whiskey bottle while having "a wild party" with her and "a woman in black." The Marion

County Sheriff's Office took his confession "with a grain of salt," and gave both he and his former wife polygraph examinations. In addition, the sheriff scheduled Luallen for a psychiatric evaluation.

The polygraph examiner detected no deception in Mrs. Luallen's statement that she was not involved in the Ridings murder. At the same time, he found deception in Bill Luallen's statement that he was involved in the killing.

During the 10 years following the slaying of Maoma Ridings at least a dozen people, including Bill Luallen, confessed to the murder but all were cleared by investigation. This murder was never solved.

Bill Luallen was released from the Indiana State Penitentiary at Michigan City and returned to Brushy Mountain State Prison at Petros on December 2, 1949. He escaped from custody again on February 9, 1951 after being moved from Brushy Mountain to a Loudon County work camp. Luallen was captured by the FBI in Davenport, Iowa on April 7, 1951, a week following the murder of Mary Hankins.

At the time of his arrest in Iowa, Luallen was in possession of a blue 1950 Ford stolen at Nashville, Tennessee for which he had purchased tags from the Campbell County Clerk, Jacksboro, Tennessee on the morning of March 31st, the day of the murder.

Luallen was convicted of a federal Dyer Act violation (interstate transportation of a stolen motor vehicle) and served a federal sentence at the U. S. Penitentiary in Atlanta. He was released from federal custody in November 1953 and returned to Brushy Mountain. His term was set to expire on February 9, 1957, but he was eligible for parole on February 9, 1955.

Atlanta Federal Penitentiary Circa 1960

The only known connection between Luallen and Indianapolis was an older brother, Roy Von Luallen, who moved from Knoxville to Indianapolis but returned to Knoxville years later. No ties to Nashville at the time the 1950 Ford was stolen or to Davenport, Iowa when it was recovered were unearthed during the search for details of these events.

In mid-November, 1954, Floyd Bruce, a Knoxville bootlegger, who had been jailed for prowling by the Knoxville Police Department after being found behind a Western Avenue business, furnished information implicating Luallen in the Hankins murder. Bruce told Knoxville Detective Bernard Waggoner and others that at about 5:00 p.m. on the day of the Hankins murder he delivered 18 pints of whiskey to Buford Roberts at his home on Rudy Street (located some five miles north of downtown at the foot of Sharp's Ridge).

Shortly after he arrived, while standing in the front yard, Bill Luallen came walking around the rear of the house. Bruce saw no car anywhere nearby and assumed that Luallen had walked through the field behind the house. Luallen was wearing a light blue shirt and light-colored pants. Both the shirt and the pants had blood on them, but no mention was made of the blood by anyone.

Roberts wanted Bruce to take Luallen to his mother's place downtown, but Bruce didn't want to do it as his car was still loaded with bootleg liquor. Roberts then said he would drive him downtown.

Floyd Bruce   **Buford Roberts**

Bruce had another conversation about Luallen with Roberts a week or so later, and Roberts told him that Luallen's family had gotten money together to get Luallen out of town. He quoted Roberts as saying, "He killed that Hankins woman as sure as anything."

The subject of Luallen's involvement in the Hankins murder came up another time when both where serving sentences between 1951 and 1954 at Brushy Mountain. During a conversation in the prison's boiler room, Roberts told Bruce that he (Roberts) had heard Luallen murdered Mrs. Hankins. Bruce also reportedly knew that Luallen had stolen a .32 caliber pistol following his escape and shortly before the Hankins' slaying.

Waggoner and others were suspicious of Bruce's information because he had never been cooperative in the past and questioned why he was now coming forward about this murder. In fact, Waggoner was quoted as saying, "I wouldn't believe Bruce though. He has never talked to us freely. This is the first time he has said anything."

Nothing was uncovered concerning Bruce's motive for coming forward with the information about Luallen. His motive could have been for revenge, a dislike of Luallen or one of his family members, or any number of reasons. The most likely impetus spurring his cooperation was the reward started by Sheriff Jones with a $100 donation.

Although the last figure publicized was $2,000, the reward pledges had, according to a Hankins' relative, actually reached the $20,000 plateau, a substantial amount of cash in 1954. Bruce's crimes – bootlegging, writing and cashing fraudulent checks, and the like – were non-violent and cash-driven. The possibility of collecting a cash reward at the end seemed the most likely reason to explain Bruce's help.

Luallen was brought to Knoxville from Brushy Mountain at the request of Attorney General Hal Clements, Jr. He was questioned on November 17, 1954 on the fourth floor of the Knox County Jail by detectives of the Knox County Sheriff's Office and Assistant Attorney General Mack Blackburn. Neither reporters from *The Knoxville Journal* nor *The Knoxville News-Sentinel* were successful in extracting a lot of detailed information from any of the detectives or Blackburn. All were apparently under strict orders to remain tight-lipped.

The only comment that Sheriff Austin Cate would make was "We've been working on this case two years." Blackburn issued a similar terse statement, saying "we are only tracking down a lead. I have nothing further to say." Even the jailor when asked if Luallen was in the jail replied, "I don't know a thing about it."

Everyone was non-committal except Bruce who had been interviewed by both papers at the city jail and had talked freely. Some information was released while some appeared to have been leaked. (Some sources were cited; others were not.)

According to Blackburn, Luallen "just laughed" when asked to give an account of his whereabouts on the day of the Hankins murder. Luallen did admit that during the time he was on the loose from prison during February, March, and April 1951 that he was in possession of a blue 1950 Ford. This, however, was an established fact as he had served almost three years in federal prison in Atlanta for transporting this stolen car from Nashville to Davenport, Iowa.

No conflicting information arose about the car, but there was conflicting information about the .32 caliber revolver alleged to have been in his possession during the time in question. *The Journal* reported that Luallen admitted having stolen a .32 caliber pistol from a Knoxville house following his escape.

The News-Sentinel reported that Luallen admitted to taking a .32 caliber Smith & Wesson revolver from the residence of Rufus Wilson, a prison official at the Loudon County work camp from which he escaped in early February 1951 but that this gun was returned to Wilson by Luallen's mother prior to the Hankins murder. Wilson told sheriff deputies he could not recall when the gun was returned. Wilson claimed that the gun was stolen again following its return by another inmate who allegedly sold the gun to a Spartanburg, South Carolina cab driver.

After spending a couple of nights in the Knox County Jail in November 1954, Luallen was returned to Brushy Mountain State Prison without being charged. He had cut off all communication with detectives and Blackburn claiming that he had received word from Brushy Mountain "to keep his mouth shut."

There were a number of Knox County Sheriff's Office detectives and deputies that worked on the Hankins case from the time it was first reported up through the attempted interview of Bill Luallen. Two of these detectives were Pat Patterson, Sr. and John M. Beeler. Patterson, in fact, handled some of the initial leads in the case and assisted in interviewing both Joseph Hegler and Bill Luallen.

During the years that followed Luallen's interview, Patterson and Beeler had conversations with a close associate and frequent "ride-along" with one of the detectives, who was also a blood relative of Mrs. Hankins. During these conversations Patterson and Beeler talked about statements made by Luallen that were not made public.

According to Patterson and Beeler, Luallen admitted that he had stolen the .32 caliber revolver that had been recovered from the creek off Norris Freeway but had refused to admit anything further about the gun. Luallen was willing to admit to larceny but not murder, saying that he could do five years for larceny but was not going to serve a murder sentence. Luallen claimed to have taken the revolver in question from the Andy Benton Grocery in Andersonville, Tennessee.

If Patterson, Beeler, or any other officers ever verified the theft of this gun from the Andy Benton Grocery, nothing was published about it. No account of the theft of this gun from Benton was published in *The Clinton Courier, The Knoxville Journal, or The Knoxville News-Sentinel* during the pertinent time frame. Unfortunately, Benton died in 1952 prior to Luallen making this claim. Had this Colt revolver been reported stolen by Benton in 1951, such a theft report would no longer be available from the Anderson County Sheriff's Department.

Benton's Grocery was located in the Mill Creek community five miles from the intersection of Norris Freeway (U. S. Highway 441) outside of Andersonville at what is now identified as 669 Mill Creek Road. The store was torn down in the late '50's or early '60's by the second owner following the Benton's. Situated behind the store was the house, which is still standing and inhabited, where the Benton's lived. The store and the house were situated on 22 acres purchased by the Benton's in late 1949 or early 1950 and which they sold on April 26, 1951, four weeks following the murder of Mrs. Hankins. The Benton's had bought this property from Reuben Pyles and sold it to Walter and Odessa Stewart.

For Luallen's claim that he stole the murder weapon from Benton's Grocery to be believable, there would have to be a reason for him to have been in such a remote area well beyond other more suitable burglary targets. Luallen, when he escaped from the work camp at Shelbyville in April, 1943, fled to Indianapolis where an older brother was living. It would be logical that following his escape from the Loudon County work camp on February 9, 1951, he would seek refuge with friends or relatives. Investigation determined that 2-3 families with the surname of Hunley, the maiden name of Luallen's mother, had lived in the immediate vicinity of this grocery store since the late 1800's. No direct relationship was established between the Mill Creek Hunley's and the Coal Creek Hunley's from whom his mother had descended.

Patterson also related to Mrs. Hankins' relative that Assistant Attorney General Blackburn was unwilling to charge Luallen in absence of a confession to the murder. Patterson made the comment that "Blackburn would have had his confession if I could have had a few minutes alone with Luallen." Patterson had the reputation of being a tough law enforcement officer.

CHAPTER 8

EVIDENTIARY OBSERVATIONS AND ANALYSIS

Under our jury system a guilty verdict requires that twelve of our peers unanimously agree beyond a reasonable doubt that the defendant committed the crime. "Reasonable doubt" is the standard that must be met. This is the requirement of our criminal statutes. Civilly, the lesser standard of "a preponderance of the evidence" is applied.

The evidence against Bill Luallen was compelling, albeit circumstantial, but was it compelling enough to satisfy our standard of reasonable doubt? Or, does the evidence fall somewhere in between the two requirements? The evidence will be examined here as well as the "how" and "why" promised in the introduction. Also, the most probable theory of and motive for the murder is presented.

Bill Luallen had sometime between his escape from the Loudon County work camp on February 9th and the day before the Hankins murder on March 31st, stolen a blue 1950 Ford at Nashville. When he was charged by the FBI in Davenport, Iowa on April 7th, it wasn't necessary to show all the dates the car may have crossed state lines in the interim between the theft of the vehicle and its recovery. The fact that it was stolen in Tennessee and was found in Iowa proved that it had traveled in interstate commerce, which was all that was necessary under the statute. Neither was it necessary for the FBI to prove that he stole the car, only that he knew it was stolen. The recency of the theft and the fact he had registered it in his name in Campbell County on March 31st was more than sufficient to prove knowledge.

The FBI investigation showed that Luallen had registered the Ford at the Campbell County Court Clerk's office in Jacksboro sometime before noon the day of the murder. The Campbell County Courthouse was just over 30 miles from the Hankins home in Harrill Hills and could easily be reached in an hour's drive.

The Hankins' neighbor, Mrs. Schumaker, in addition to being "clothes conscious," apparently was also vehicle conscious, or at least, Ford conscious. She described the car that pulled up in front of the Hankins home as a black 1950 Ford bearing Knox County tags. How many women in 1951 could state with any degree of certainty that this was a 1950 Ford? The 1950 Ford looked very much like the 1949 and the 1951. The only difference between the 1950 and the 1949 was that the 1950 had push button door handles while the 1949 had pull door handles. The only major differences between the 1950 Ford and the 1951 was the grill design and the taillight lenses. Dark blue was one of the most popular colors of 1950 Fords and could have been easily mistaken for black.

1950 Ford

Mrs. Schumaker also said that the car bore Knox County tags. How did she know that? Tennessee license plates at that time did not bear a decal with the county's name on it, but rather they bore a number, the first number, identifying the county. The number was determined by population.

Knox County was the third most populated county in the state so Knox County tags bore the number "3" to identify it as a Knox County tag. Shelby County (Memphis) tags bore the number "1" while Davidson County (Nashville) was assigned the number "2." Hamilton County (Chattanooga) tags bore the number "4" and so on. Campbell County tags bore the number "31" as the first number on the left side of the plate.

The tag could have been as easily mistaken for a Knox County tag as the dark blue color was mistaken for black.

Mrs. Schumaker, although she never made eye contact with the intruder or did she get a good enough look to be able to later identify him, was nonetheless a very good witness. One thing she certainly would have noticed would have been gloves, had the intruder been wearing any.

The killer had entered and departed through the Hankins' front door, opening it from the inside, and closing it from the outside. Since the decision had been made not to process the scene for latent fingerprints, the Knox County Sheriff's Office unfortunately had none to compare with the fingerprints of Bill Luallen when he became a suspect in November 1954.

Luallen had broken into his first house to steal over a dozen years before driving through the Harrill Hills area that March afternoon. As usual he wanted to be sure that he was entering a house where there was no one at home. He saw two people leave the Hankins house and could only be certain no one was at home by knocking on the door, which is what he did. If no one was at home he could gain entry through another door if the front door was locked. He had found that the easiest way to avoid suspicion was to act as if you belonged and had a valid reason for being there. If someone answered the door, he could use the guise of asking for directions or some other ruse that would allow him to just leave without causing alarm.

When Luallen looked through the door window and then the picture window and saw Mrs. Hankins coming to the door, he was thinking about what he was going to say. When she opened the door, he changed his mind. His thoughts of asking for directions or of using another ruse to explain his presence disappeared.

At that point there was one of two motives that crossed his mind. The first, robbery, was the reason he was there, but without anyone present. The second motive, sexual assault, either rape or forcing her to perform a sexual act, most probably entered his mind as well. He immediately found her attractive and appealing.

Luallen had been divorced for almost ten years and had been in prison almost all of that time. In fact, up until a couple of months previously, he had been incarcerated continuously for seven years – in Indiana, Atlanta, and Loudon County. And here before him was a young woman who was pure, clean, and attractive – the type woman he had not had in years, or perhaps had never had.

On the other hand the sight of the Gruen wristwatch on her arm may have been enough to tip the scale to robbery, fueling the thought that there may be other items of value inside that he could force from her. Whether one, or all these thoughts went through his mind, he decided to gain entry into the house rather than make an excuse for his knock and retreat.

Armed with the fully-loaded .32 caliber revolver, Luallen first tried to con his way into the house, but realizing that approach was not going to work, he showed her the gun and forced his way in. After walking to the hall near the top of the basement steps, Luallen made her get on her knees and forced her to perform a despicable sexual act. If she screamed, no one heard her. Neither did anyone hear the gunshot when she turned to escape his grasp, and he shot her through the top left side of her head. The shot caused blood to splatter both on his shirt and his pants. Before leaving he slipped the Gruen wristwatch off her wrist and stuck it in his pocket.

When Luallen left the Hankins' residence he could not be certain if anyone had heard anything or if anyone other than Mrs. Schumaker had seen him. He had to know that the police would soon be looking for the 1950 Ford he was driving. Luallen had to be thinking about where he could hide the car and get to someplace where he would be safe. He decided to go to Buford Roberts for help. Roberts' house was six miles away, but he stopped nearby and hid the car, then walked the rest of the way to Roberts' house.

Buford Roberts lived in a house at 412 Rudy Street NW (in 1952 the house number changed from 412 to 3353) in Knoxville, which house was actually owned by his step-father, Walter Moore and his mother, Katie. The house was located near the southern base of Sharp's Ridge off Heiskell Avenue in the Lonsdale area. Roberts' step-father worked at the Palm Beach factory on Baxter Avenue some three miles south of the residence.

Buford Roberts, like Luallen, and like Floyd Bruce, who was there when Luallen got to the house around 5:00

o'clock that afternoon, was a career criminal. He had been in and out prison over the years and had a long arrest record for burglary, armed robbery, and bootlegging. Roberts and Bruce were both 20 years older than Luallen. During the '30s and '40s Roberts had been tied to the Ernie Miller gang in Knoxville which was made up primarily of burglars, armed robbers, bootleggers, and from time to time, killers. Miller was actually from Middlesboro, Kentucky, not Knoxville, but had been associated with gangster types in Knoxville and other East Tennessee counties.

Because of his connection with Miller, Roberts had been picked up for questioning in a double homicide in Sevier County in September, 1949. Charlie Perry, a former Knoxville bootlegger, had been murdered along with his live-in housekeeper at Perry's Camp, a popular tourist court and beer joint. There was speculation that the motive for the murder could have been revenge on the part of Miller, Roberts, or other members of the gang for Perry turning in three members of the gang in 1935 in connection with the burglary of American Clothing Company on West Jackson Avenue in which apparel valued at $15,000 had been taken. Roberts had been arrested for the burglary but was released. The goods were recovered at Perry's Camp.

Roberts was also released for the Perry murders and three men were arrested and charged with the murders a couple of days later. Two of the men, Claude Robertson and Hermie Lee Jones, were later convicted and sentenced to 99 years.

Roberts and Bruce both saw the blood on Luallen's light blue shirt and light-colored pants, but there was no conversation about the blood, at least, not in Bruce's presence. In addition to the car, the intruder's dress described by Mrs. Schumaker generally matched that of Bruce's description of Luallen's dress.

Bruce was at Roberts house delivering bootleg liquor, still had liquor in his car, and did not want to drive Luallen downtown to his mother's residence. Roberts, by doing so, again became an accessory after the fact just as he had been in the Grant murder the year before. Luallen's mother, Harriet, was at the time living in an apartment in the 400 block of Locust Street near Union Avenue. Luallen's father, Dallas, and his youngest brother, Jack B. Luallen, were both living in apartments at 1317 5th Avenue Northwest, which was much closer to Rudy Street than Locust Avenue downtown. His father was still working at Southern Railroad and Jack, who had gotten married, had also gotten a job at Southern as a coach cleaner. Other members of the Luallen family were living with Dallas.

A week later Roberts would tell Bruce that Luallen's family had gotten some money together to get him out of town. It was then that Roberts made the statement, "He killed that Hankins woman as sure as anything." Luallen was arrested in Davenport, Iowa with the stolen car at about the same time Roberts and Bruce were having this conversation.

Another of Luallen's brothers, Daniel Leon, who was seven years older than Bill, was serving a 99-year sentence at Brushy Mountain for the murder in Roane County of prominent Roane County contractor, Robert N. Grant, on March 21, 1950. Leon had been arrested three days later and subsequently indicted for murder along with two other men – Clyde Sands and Eddie Rudder. He was tried and convicted in June 1950.

Leon had reportedly been a member of the Clarence Bunch gang that terrorized several East Tennessee counties during the early 1930s. Bunch who was from Claiborne County, Tennessee, and fancied himself a John Dellinger, was killed in a shootout with Knox County officers in August 1934.

Leon Luallen

Leon, known as "Big Lu," had been imprisoned for a 1931 conviction for housebreaking and larceny and a 1934 car theft conviction, receiving a three-year sentence for each offense. He was pardoned by Governor Gordon Browning in January 1937 two days before Browning left his first term of office.

Sands, known as "Ikey," who also received a 99-year sentence, had been paroled less than 90 days before the Grant murder. He had been convicted, along with fellow Knoxvillians Bill Rowland and Chip Bailey, in the 1935 murder of Knoxville druggist George Harrison, and had been sentenced to life imprisonment.

Eddie Rudder, age 19 at the time of the Grant murder, was sentenced to 20 years in return for his cooperation and testimony against Luallen and Sands.

Rudder had been recruited to drive Luallen and Sands the night of the planned robbery and murder of Grant by Buford Roberts and had been introduced to Luallen the day before by Roberts. Roberts had asked Rudder if he was interested in making some easy money, perhaps as much as

$7,000-$8,000. Roberts loaned his car to Rudder for use in the robbery.

As a result, Roberts was held initially as a material witness on a $10,000 bond. He was arrested and charged in connection with the murder during the trial of Luallen and Sands during which Rudder testified as to the role played by Roberts. According to Rudder, Roberts furnished his black 1941 Cadillac, gas money, and two pistols.

Roberts, already in custody as a material witness, was thereafter charged with accessory before the fact to homicide. He was tried and convicted on September 14, 1950 and was sentenced to 20 years and one day.

**Clyde Sands, Knoxville Homicide Captain
Jim Wilkerson, and Eddie Rudder**

There were some intriguing side notes concerning Roberts' trial in the Grant case in Roane County. While he was in Roane County jail awaiting trial, his 69-year-old mother, Katie Moore, and his 20-year-old step-sister were arrested in Knoxville for transporting moonshine whiskey. Renown Knoxville defense attorney Ray Jenkins, hired by Grant's widow as a special prosecutor to prosecute all the defendants in the case, argued, of course, for the State at Roberts' trial.

In his closing argument Jenkins cited a long list of convictions in Roberts' criminal record and asserted "whatever crimes this man has committed in his long history of law-breaking, the most dastardly was having his 69-year-old mother and his lovely young sister carry on his dirty business while he was in jail." Roberts had been dubbed "the arch criminal of East Tennessee" during the course of his trial at Kingston.

Roberts was released on bond pending the appeal of his conviction which explains his being at home when Bill Luallen came to the Rudy Street house on the day of the Hankins murder. Roberts' conviction, like those of Leon Luallen and Clyde Sands, was affirmed by the Superior Court of Tennessee at Knoxville. He was taken into custody once again by the Roane County Sheriff on July 13, 1951 and thereafter transferred to Brushy Mountain.

Leon Luallen, who exhausted all avenues of his appeals available to him in both state and federal courts by 1972, would spend another six years in prison before being released from the Tennessee State Penitentiary in Nashville during the corruption-plagued administration of Governor Ray Blanton. He remarried following his release and lived in Nashville and Knoxville until 1995. He spent most of his last days in a Knoxville nursing home. He died in February, 1995 in Orlando, Florida.

During the time Leon was in the Nashville Penitentiary, he, like other inmates during the 1950s and 1960s, became a prolific songwriter. Leon, like other white inmates, wrote rockabilly and country while the black inmates for the most part wrote rhythm and blues and rock and roll tunes. Two of the songs written by Leon – "Polka on the Banjo" and "Don't Bug Me Baby" – were recorded by several well-known artists including Lester Flatt and Earl Scruggs, Red Foley, and Chet Atkins.

Shortly before Bill Luallen was brought to Knoxville from Brushy Mountain Prison for questioning in November 1954, Jack B. Luallen, the youngest of the Luallen men, had been convicted in Knoxville of beating a stranger to death with a coffee mug during an argument at a Depot Avenue café. Jack, like his father and another older brother, had gotten a job with Southern Railroad and worked near this café cleaning Southern passenger cars at the railroad depot. His conviction resulted in his being the third Luallen brother incarcerated in a Tennessee prison.

Leon Luallen at the time of his arrest in March, 1950 was living at 812 Belle Aire Avenue in the Western Heights neighborhood near Mechanicsville. Dallas, Jack, and two of Jack's sisters lived in the nearby Old North Knoxville area. Bill Luallen had previously lived on May Avenue in this neighborhood. These addresses were all located within two miles of Fred Hankins' business, Construction Services, Inc., at Chavannes Lumber Company, located near Southern Railroad's Coster Shops where Dallas Luallen worked.

Bill Luallen's familiarity with the area suggests the possibility he may have somehow learned the address of the Hankins' new residence and targeted it for robbery. Or, which is more likely, he simply drove through Harrill Hills and cased the neighborhood en route from Jacksboro to downtown Knoxville. That was, after all, what he had done for years when not in prison.

The only item taken from the Hankins crime scene was Mrs. Hankins' wristwatch. Was this watch taken as a memento, as a piece of property to sell, or as a gift for someone? Since there was no evidence of sexual assault, and

Luallen's *modus operandi* was to steal for cash, it appears more likely the watch was taken to sell or as a gift.

The problem with trying to sell it was the same problem that existed with the car – the police would be looking for it. He had no way of knowing that disseminating information about the watch would fall through the cracks and not be done on a timely basis. Like the 1950 Ford, the Gruen wristwatch was also "hot" (not just stolen, but murder evidence). If the watch was subsequently pawned, it was most likely pawned at an out-of-town or even an out-of-state pawn shop.

The most probable disposition of the watch was to give it to someone as a gift. The most likely recipient of this gift would have been the person whose help he sought that late March afternoon – his mother, Harriet Luallen.

The evidence regarding the murder weapon and its history is the most amazing, confusing, and coincidental of all – all at the same time. The .32 caliber Colt revolver discovered in the creek alongside Norris Freeway three and one-half months after the murder was identified by the FBI Laboratory as the murder weapon based on a comparison of the slug removed from Mrs. Hankins' head with the five unspent cartridges remaining in the pistol when recovered. Even though the analysis used by the FBI to effect this identification was years later abandoned by the laboratory, the accompanying circumstantial evidence supports the conclusion that this was the murder weapon.

According to information related to Mrs. Hankins' relative by Patterson and Beeler, Bill Luallen admitted stealing this .32 revolver from the Andy Benton Grocery in Andersonville but admitted to nothing beyond stealing the gun. There is no corroboration of this admission – only the conversations had between Knox County Sheriff's detectives

Pat Patterson, Sr. and John M. Beeler with a close relative of Mrs. Hankins. The origin or theft of this gun could not be established in 1954 or 2010. Bill Luallen admitted to Detective Pat Patterson that he stole the murder weapon during the burglary of Benton's Grocery but never admitted throwing it in the creek off Norris Freeway. To have done so would have arguably put him in possession of the gun after the murder.

Perhaps the most astounding coincidence in this case, as told to Mrs. Hankins' relative by Patterson and Beeler, had to do with the origin of the murder weapon.

Andrew "Andy" William Benton born and raised in McMinn County, Tennessee, married Vada Arnwine from the Corryton community. Benton had worked in Knoxville but lived in Corryton. He and his wife had lived near and had attended the same church as the Hankins and the Tablers – Graveston Baptist – where Mary Hankins' funeral was later held.

According to a relative of Clyde Woods, Benton worked as a Knox County deputy sheriff in the administration of Sheriff Wesley Brewer who served two terms as sheriff from 1932-1936. He has been described by Woods' relative as "one of those badge carrying deputies," also known as a "fee grabber."

Benton, along with his partner, Clyde Woods, "fee grabbed" black buyers of bootleg whiskey on Central Avenue in downtown Knoxville during the 1930s while working under Brewer. Either Benton or Woods would pose as a bootlegger along Central Avenue and sell an unsuspecting black buyer bootleg whiskey. The buyer would almost immediately be arrested by the other officer and taken before Squire John Parker whose office was located on State Street a few blocks away. Squire Parker would fine the buyer

$5.00 which would later be split three ways between Benton, Woods, and Parker.

During the '40s Andy Benton bought the grocery store in Andersonville, and he and his wife moved to Andersonville. Benton died in 1952 and his wife moved to Tampa, Florida, where she died in 1970. The theft of the gun was never verified. It was learned, however, that Andy Benton had come into possession of this gun in the early 1940's when he purchased his first grocery store in Corryton from James. E. Hankins, father of Fred Hankins, and father-in-law of the victim, Mary Hankins.

According to the Hankins relative, "the gun came with the store." Benton took the gun with him to Andersonville after he sold the Corryton store previously owned by Hankins. James E. Hankins, after selling his grocery store to Benton, opened his furniture store in Fountain City. The murder weapon having previously passed through the hands of the victim's father-in-law was an incredible coincidence, but there is no evidence to indicate it was anything other than a coincidence.

No information is now available to allow the .32 caliber Colt revolver sold new in Sevier County in 1914 to be traced to James E. Hankins. Neither is there is list of suspects available whose known fingerprints were compared to the latent fingerprints found on the cartridges in the murder weapon. This aspect of the investigation was never publicized. No suspects' names whose prints were compared to the murder weapon were ever released.

The prints of those initially detained, Joseph Hegler, Bill Luallen, Andy Benton, and James Hankins should have all been compared to the prints on the cartridges. Had this been done, and the prints matched with one of these men, that information would have become known in the public domain, but this never happened. The cartridges could have been put in the revolver's chamber by someone other than any of these men and remained in the gun for a long period of time. This aspect of the investigation, regrettably, is an unsolvable mystery.

The claims made in connection with the second .32 caliber revolver, reported to be a Smith & Wesson, are not believable. Luallen claimed to have stolen this pistol following his escape on February 9th from the Loudon work camp. He claimed to have taken it from the residence of Rufus Wilson, a prison official at the work camp. Luallen's mother claims that she returned this .32 caliber revolver to Wilson prior to Hankins murder, but Wilson did not remember when she returned it. Wilson did remember the gun was stolen again by another inmate who sold it to a cab driver in Spartanburg, South Carolina. This account was reported in *The Knoxville News-Sentinel* on November 18, 1954 while Luallen was at the Knox County Jail for questioning.

The Harriman Record in its weekly issue of February 15, 1951, had reported on the circumstances surrounding the theft of Wilson's pistol by Luallen at the time of his escape from the Loudon County work camp on Friday, February 9th. According to this account, written less than a week following the escape, Luallen escaped from the road gang by overpowering Wilson and taking his pistol. Luallen had boasted before his escape that he was going to go to Kingston and "break Leon out of jail." Leon Luallen had not yet been taken to Brushy Mountain State Prison to begin his 99-year sentence for the murder of Robert Grant and was still being housed in the Roane County Jail in Kingston.

On the same day *The News-Sentinel* reported the claims regarding the handgun allegedly stolen by Luallen from Wilson, an account in *The Knoxville Journal* reported,

"It was learned while he was free, Luallen broke into a Knoxville house and stole a .32 caliber pistol—the same caliber weapon used in the murder." The next day *The Journal* reported that Floyd Bruce had told Knoxville Detective Chief Bernard Waggoner that Luallen while in escape status had stolen a .32 caliber pistol shortly before the Hankins murder. Chief Waggoner, who was skeptical of Bruce, was quoted as saying, "I don't know how he knew about it, but he did."

After weeding through all the information reported about the .32 caliber revolvers, it appears most likely the revolver that Floyd Bruce told Chief Waggoner about was the revolver Luallen admitted stealing from Benton's Grocery, the same revolver recovered near Bull Run Creek and later identified by the FBI as the murder weapon.

Unfortunately, the investigation of the Hankins murder was botched from beginning to end. It reeked of unprofessionalism and ineptness. But as previously pointed out, this was a different time. It was a good time to be a defense attorney.

The Hankins case would have been an ideal case for Ray Jenkins to have served as a special prosecutor. Jenkins had been involved with several cases as a retained prosecutor during his career. He had prosecuted the Grant case in Roane County and was familiar with the players – the Luallen family, Buford Roberts, and their associates. He had represented more Knox County murder defendants than anyone else. Before Jenkins' career came to an end he had represented more than 600 alleged murderers.

"The Terror of Tellico Plains" had just returned to his Knoxville law practice after serving as Chief Counsel for the U. S. Senate Investigations Subcommittee in the feud between Senator Joseph R. McCarthy and the Army. He had been appointed in April, 1954 amid accolades from friends and rivals. Mayor Dempster, a Democrat, described Jenkins, a Republican, as "one of the finest lawyers practicing in Tennessee." Fellow attorneys and court officials rated him as one of Knoxville's finest trial lawyers. One unidentified Knoxville resident was quoted as saying, "when people get in trouble around here they think of Ray Jenkins first. With him on their side, they figure the other side is behind the eight-ball to start with."

By June, 1954 "Draft Ray Jenkins" captions were appearing in Tennessee newspapers between East Tennessee and Nashville, but Jenkins ultimately rejected the Republican nomination bid to run for the U. S. Senate. Instead, he returned to his law practice full-time in October, and on the political front, supported his friend, U. S. Representative Howard Baker, in his re-election bid to Congress. Had Jenkins run for the U. S. Senate, his Democratic opponent would have been Senator Estes Kefauver of Madisonville.

Ray Jenkins

Ray Jenkins would have been as good a fit to ferret out the truth in this case and to seek justice for Mary Hankins as he had been to handle the McCarthy investigation. Had Jenkins been the prosecutor, one of the greatest judicial advocates in Knox County history would have been at Mrs. Hankins' side and at her table with Attorney General Clements in the event of a trial. This also would have eliminated the possibility of this great legal mind and courtroom phenomenon being at the opposing table with the defendant.

Ray Jenkins most likely followed the developments in the Hankins murder with great interest. It is unfortunate that he never played an active, major role in the case.

CHAPTER 9

ADDITIONAL CORROBORATING EVIDENCE

The *modus operandi* of Bill Luallen never varied. He robbed homeowners of their personal possessions when no one was at home. He stole items that were easy to carry, had marketable value, and could easily be fenced in the black market or sold at pawn shops.

During the times between prison terms he stuck to stealing from houses during the daytime when the occupants were at work or whom he knew to be absent. When he was caught and charged, the charge was always the same – House Breaking and Larceny.

The only other charge was Auto Larceny. This was his first offense when he was 16 years old and sentenced to the Tennessee State Reformatory in Nashville. In 1962 he rented a car in Knoxville using an alias, kept the car, and was subsequently charged with Larceny after Trust. All of his other arrests were daytime home burglaries.

Luallen's favorite takes from his burglaries, i. e., the items of property he most frequently sought and stole, were guns of any kind, watches of any kind, and, of course, cash. This can best be demonstrated by summarizing the larcenies he committed following his paroles in 1955, 1959, and 1962.

After being returned from the Atlanta Federal Penitentiary to Brushy Mountain in November, 1953 to finish the sentence imposed in Knox County in 1942, Luallen was paroled on February 9, 1955 - three months after being brought to Knoxville for interrogation concerning the Hankins murder. Almost eight months later in September

Luallen was indicted in Davidson County for four daytime house burglaries committed during May and June, 1955 in the south Nashville area. Luallen pled guilty to all these charges and on September 28th received a three-year sentence to run concurrently in each case.

The total value of the items taken in these four burglaries was $3,100. The property taken in these thefts consisted of six shotguns, three rifles, two handguns, six watches, and miscellaneous other items including cash. Five of the six watches taken were stolen in one burglary.

Luallen was returned to Brushy Mountain on September 30, 1955 but was paroled again on July 8, 1959. In January, 1960 Luallen was indicted for two more daytime burglaries that occurred in Lake City in Anderson County on October 22, 1959. Luallen was familiar with Lake City as both his parents were both born in the community which later became Lake City, and he had a half-brother, Otha Hunley, who lived there. Additionally, one of the victims in these cases was Lawrence H. Luallen, an electrical engineer at TVA. Although no kinship was substantiated, Bill Luallen had used the alias, Larry Luallen, in Indiana in 1944.

Among the property stolen by Luallen in these two thefts was a rifle, a handgun, four watches, other miscellaneous items, and cash having a value of more than $1,000. Luallen, who pled guilty to the charges, was sentenced on February 4, 1960 to three years on each charge to be served consecutively with credit for time served since his arrest in October. He was returned to Brushy Mountain a week later.

Luallen was again paroled on October 11, 1962 and was returned from parole, again as with the two previous paroles, with a new sentence, on February 23, 1963. The reason for his return from parole was three new charges that occurred in December, 1962 and January, 1963 in Knox County. The three indictments involved two housebreaking and larceny cases while the third related to larceny after trust which involved Luallen's rental of an Avis rental car under the alias Virgil Andrew Luallen which he never returned. These two burglaries, both committed in west Knox County, netted Luallen no guns, but he did take a watch in each. Luallen pled guilty to all three indictments and received a three-year sentence in each case to run concurrently.

Bill Luallen was last paroled from Brushy Mountain on July 4, 1965, and incredibly, never returned to the Tennessee prison system. From age 18 to 45, Luallen had spent less than three years collectively on the street. This less than three year accumulation of time consisted of two periods he was in escape status and three periods when he was on parole. He had served time not only in the Tennessee prison system but had also done hard time in the Indiana State Penitentiary at Michigan City, Indiana and at the Atlanta Federal Penitentiary.

CHAPTER 10

EVIDENCE SUGGESTING AND DISPROVING FAMILY INVOLVEMENT

Tying the murder weapon to the victim's father-in-law in this case came as an unbelievable coincidence, or revelation, depending on interpretation of the evidence and events. It must be remembered that this information is hearsay, decades old, and can neither be corroborated nor disproved. Unfortunately, Detectives Patterson and Beeler are no longer among us and haven't been for several years. Neither are their files. The source of this information concerning the lineage of the murder weapon has been found to be entirely reliable, so there is no doubt that Patterson and Beeler related the information. The reliability issue thus transfers to the reliability of Patterson and Beeler.

Pat Patterson, Sr. was known to be a no-nonsense, tough police officer. That didn't mean he was dishonest or unfair. It meant he was allowed to go by a different set of rules than those that have become so familiar in the 21st century world. The Miranda case, mandating law enforcement's duty to advise custodial suspects of their constitutional right against self-incrimination and their right to an attorney, was not decided until 1966. The absence of this decision had afforded law enforcement officers more latitude in the interrogation of suspects. There was no reason, however, to question Patterson's veracity.

John M. Beeler, a Corryton resident, Patterson's partner, and an even closer associate and friend of the Hankins' relative, was, some 20 years after the interrogation of Bill Luallen, convicted of criminal acts that would have caused his credibility to be challenged. Beeler, elected Knox County Commissioner of Welfare in 1970 and re-elected in 1974, was charged and convicted in the late 1970's in federal district court at Knoxville of obstructing, delaying and affecting commerce by extortion in violation of the Hobbs Act. These charges were brought amid allegations that Beeler had extorted $117,500 between 1972 and 1975 from a waste management company in return for his favorable vote on a proposed landfill. His first conviction was reversed on appeal on the ground of variance between the indictment and the evidence in 1978. Beeler was retried, however, and was convicted a second time of charges brought in a new indictment. He received a prison sentence of four years. The case was again appealed but his conviction was affirmed by the appellate court in 1981.

Even though Beeler's conviction might cause some to question his integrity, there is no reason to believe that either he or Patterson would have been anything other than truthful with the Hankins relative. They had no reason to lie, but had every reason to relate the truth. They wanted the Hankins family and relatives to know as many details about the alleged involvement of Bill Luallen in Mary Hankins' death as they could determine. Their relationship with the family discouraged them from lying.

Tying the Colt revolver to the victim's father-in-law was something that Patterson and Beeler could have done with the admission from Luallen that he stole the gun from Benton's Grocery. Beeler, being a resident of Corryton, very likely knew about the gun that had gone from James E. Hankins to Andy Benton. Or, if no personal knowledge, it was the kind of thing that either Patterson or Beeler could have determined very easily.

In view of the preceding, there is a great probability that the information concerning the murder weapon is entirely true. However, there is no evidence to prove that the victim's husband or father-in-law had anything to do with the victim's murder simply because her father-in-law at one time owned the murder weapon. There is no reason to believe that this is anything other than an almost unbelievable coincidence.

Aside from the fact the murder weapon was once owned by Mrs. Hankins' father-in-law, there are other facts that cause suspicion to raise its head and point a finger at Fred Hankins. The first that comes to mind is his being gone from home that Saturday afternoon for what could have been a pre-arranged time frame.

Hankins apparently had made an appointment to have repairs or maintenance work to be performed on his car at Hensley Motor Service and after picking up his car spent time visiting his father whose business was across the street from Hensley. This could also explain the ease with which Luallen entered the house, described by Mrs. Schumaker as being no longer that a 12-count, before he was let in by Mrs. Hankins. Luallen could have said something indicating he knew where Mr. Hankins was, that he had business with him, and would wait for his return.

Had such a pre-arranged scheme existed between Luallen and Fred Hankins, it makes no sense, however, that Luallen would have come to the Hankins' home with a .32 caliber Colt revolver, a loud, noisy weapon likely to be heard, rather than a knife to stab her or cord with which to strangle her to death. These facts do not support a pre-meditated murder for hire.

Another action on the part of Fred Hankins that raised suspicion at the time he returned home to find his wife dying from a gunshot wound to her head was his running next door to tell his next door neighbors, the Holts, that his wife had been shot and rely on them to call an ambulance and the sheriff's office. Why did he not call immediately from his home? Was this an intentional effort on his part to delay medical attention or was it the excitement and stressfulness of the moment that caused him to react the way he did?

In view of his demeanor during later questioning and the days and weeks that followed, it became apparent his initial reaction was simply one of overwhelming anxiety and hysteria. Mr. Hankins was so incoherent, sobbing uncontrollably, following the discovery of his wife that he could hardly talk to the sheriff and his investigators. He moved out the house to his parents' home just blocks away following the murder and sold it within a matter of months. His demeanor and behavior was not that of a cold-blooded contract killer.

There are other facts that effectively quash the notion of a contract killing, but the single most significant fact is that the shooter, whether Bill Luallen or someone else, committed the murder with a gun. If a hit man had been paid to kill Mrs. Hankins, even the dumbest hit man would not have used a weapon that was possibly going to be heard. He could have very easily have stabbed or strangled her death. Had the killer been bent on using a gun, he could have very easily procured a silencer, homemade or otherwise.

Although most of the Luallen family lived within a two-mile radius of Fred Hankins' office, there was no reason to believe that any of the Luallen's knew any of the Hankins. Additionally, Bill Luallen had, up until the month before the murder, been in prison for seven years. Most of that time had been served in Indiana. The Hankins' house was in Fountain City over six miles away from the nearest Luallen family member.

Two other facts that sway suspicion away from Fred Hankins and his father are the victim's watch and the financing of Luallen's flight from Knoxville following the murder. Mrs. Hankins' Gruen wristwatch was taken during the murder but was not noticed or reported by her husband until 2-3 days later. Had he or a member of his family been part of a murder conspiracy, it is very unlikely that he would have shared that information with the sheriff's office since anyone caught with the watch might be tied to the murder. The single most convincing fact that exonerates the Hankins, however, is that Luallen's family raised money to effect his flight from Knoxville. Had this been a contract murder, Luallen would have had the money to leave town right away.

All these facts support the conclusion reached by Patterson and Beeler, as reported to the Hankins relative, that the murder of Mary Hankins was committed as the result of a bungled daylight house burglary.

CHAPTER 11

CONCLUSION AND AUTHOR'S COMMENTS

The evidence suggests the conclusion that Bill Luallen is the most likely suspect to have murdered Mary Hankins. He had no motive, only fear of being caught and sent back to prison. The most logical explanation for this senseless murder is that Luallen panicked when Mrs. Hankins, after succumbing to his demands at gunpoint to perform a sexual act, turned to free herself from his grasp. Rather than allow her to flee from her house to summon help, Luallen shot her in the head. The fact that Luallen was inside the house for 20 minutes or so implies that he was successful in his efforts to force an unwanted sexual act upon Mrs. Hankins.

Luallen's journey to the Hankins' home had begun almost two months previously. He had "escaped" from the Loudon County work camp on the 9th of February. During the 45-plus days since that time he had stolen a 1950 Ford at Nashville and had just that morning before driving to Harrill Hills purchased a tag for the car at the Campbell County Courthouse in Jacksboro. At some time during his suspected stay in the Mill Creek community he had burglarized Andy Benton's grocery store and stolen Benton's .32 caliber Colt revolver. He may even have stolen the revolver the night before the murder.

The likelihood that Luallen had stolen Benton's handgun shortly before the murder is supported by the fact he had it on his person. He had stolen hundreds of guns over the years and had sold them for profit. None of his previous crimes involved the use of a firearm. He was not a stick-up man or killer. He was a thief. He stole guns, watches, and money from empty houses. Benton's revolver, later identified by the FBI Laboratory as the murder weapon, would be recovered near Bull Run Creek off Norris Freeway two and one-half months following the murder.

When Luallen arrived in the Harrill Hills neighborhood that Saturday, it is very likely that he observed two people depart the Hankins' home in the Hankins' car. Mrs. Hankins was not outside of the house when they left. The young Hensley employee, Don Severance, would later tell investigators that he saw Mrs. Hankins inside the house through a window when they left to return to Hensley Motor Service. Depending on his vantage point, it is unlikely that Luallen could tell with certainty that there was a man and a woman in the car as opposed to two men.

When Luallen pulled up and parked in front of the Hankins' home that afternoon, he saw no evidence of anyone at home when he got out and walked to the front door. After knocking he peered through the small windows in the door and then through the picture window to the side. He saw Mary Hankins coming to the door. When she opened the door, and he saw her, he probably had thoughts of sexual gratification. After all, he was 30 years of age, and he had been in prison for the past seven years. He knew right away that he wanted more from her than the Gruen watch on her wrist. He decided not to tell her he was looking for someone who lived in the area, had knocked on her door by mistake, needed directions, or any other number of excuses that would have allowed him to back away.

Luallen at this point did one of two things, or both, to gain entry into the Hankins' home as quickly as he did. The most viable option was a combination of the two. He initially attempted to fast-talk his way through the door, but when Mrs. Hankins balked, he showed her the gun and forced his way through the door. This would explain Mrs. Schumaker's estimate of "you couldn't have counted to twelve before the man entered the house after he knocked."

Since Luallen's motive had changed from robbery to sexual assault after seeing her, he made his intentions known to Mrs. Hankins almost immediately and ordered her to her knees at gunpoint. At that point he forced her to perform a sexual act, an act for which no evidence would later be found by the coroner as use of DNA forensic analysis at crime scenes was still 40 years away. Since according to the neighbor, Mrs. Schumaker, Luallen would be inside the home for 20 minutes or so before hurriedly leaving, there is reason to believe Mrs. Hankins submitted to his demands.

After a few minutes, however, realizing she was probably going to die, she turned in an effort to escape down the basement steps. In a sudden panic, he shot her. It was at this point – while she was still on her knees – not in a prone position as theorized by Knox County Coroner Sidney Wolfenbarger, that Luallen shot her. Wolfenbarger may have had a different opinion had he known that Luallen would show up at Buford Roberts' house an hour later with blood splatter above and below his waist. The bullet entered the top left of her head and lodged just behind her right eye.

Luallen left immediately, thinking that the shot had surely been heard by a neighbor or neighbors. Before leaving, however, he stooped down and removed the Gruen watch from Mary Hankins' wrist. His taking the watch was a tell-tale clue that Luallen was responsible for the murder. He had stolen and pawned hundreds of watches over the years – Elgin, Bulova, Hamilton, Gruen, and other popular brands of the times. He had a penchant for watches in the same way that he had an affinity for guns. The temptation to take the watch, even in view of what had just happened, was too great to pass up. He could not resist.

Luallen departed the Hankins' residence as described by Mrs. Schumaker and drove to the vicinity of Buford Roberts' house on Rudy Street. He hid the car a safe distance away so as not to be seen in it and made his way to the house from the rear. He found Roberts and Floyd Bruce, two old bootleggers whom he had also known at Brushy Mountain, around front. Roberts and Bruce saw blood splatter on both Luallen's shirt and pants, which generally matched the description provided by Mrs. Schumaker, corroborating the notion that Mrs. Hankins was shot while on her knees rather than lying down. Roberts, in a conversation with Bruce a few days later, would express the opinion that Luallen killed Mrs. Hankins. A year or so later they would have a similar conversation while both were incarcerated at Brushy Mountain.

Roberts, whose car had been used by Luallen's brother, Leon, and two others, a year before when Roane County contractor Robert Grant was killed, drove Luallen to his mother's apartment in downtown Knoxville. According to Roberts during the week that followed, Luallen's family raised money for him to flee Knoxville and avoid detection and arrest. Luallen was arrested a week later in Davenport, Iowa in possession of the stolen 1950 Ford. Luallen, when brought from Brushy Mountain to Knoxville in November, 1954 admitted to Knox County Sheriff detectives that he stole the murder weapon but would not admit to the murder.

Luallen served 30 months in Atlanta for the stolen car and was returned to Brushy Mountain to serve out the remainder of the original sentence handed out in Knox County in 1942. Ironically, he was never charged with escape for leaving the Loudon County work camp in February, 1951, nor was any time added to his sentence. Whether in escape status or on parole, prisons in Tennessee, Indiana, and Georgia served as revolving doors for Luallen. When in prison, Luallen, who completed the 6th grade, worked as a baker. The only known job he had outside the walls was at the Little Dutch Pastry Shop in Nashville for three months in 1962 while out on parole. He never had a residence of his own when he was not in prison. He used his mother's address, which for a long time was 224 State Street, Apartment 1, in downtown Knoxville, as his address of record.

There has never been any credible evidence developed to implicate anyone other than Bill Luallen in the death of Mary Hankins. The suspects named initially were the result of newspaper speculation and family finger-pointing. The Hegler arrest was not only the unfortunate result of a woman scorned, but also of a political fiasco, just one of many that marred Knoxville's political landscape during that era. Knox County's Attorney General, Hal H. Clements, Jr., and his Assistant Attorney General, Mack Blackburn, however, never brought charges against Luallen, opting not to do so in absence of a confession. Had the Hankins family and/or the Tabler family procured the services of Ray Jenkins as a special prosecutor, this case would very likely have reached a different conclusion. Jenkins knew all the players, having successfully prosecuted Leon Luallen, Roberts, and two other defendants for the Grant killing in Roane County the year before the Hankins murder.

What happened at the Hankins' Harrill Hills home on the last Saturday in March, 1951, was not a pretty sight. But murder never is. The senselessness of this killing made it particularly hard to take. The family had to endure the pain of this tragedy for the rest of their lives. There was never any real closure. It was a void, a question mark, a mystery that was always present and unexplainable. The examination of the evidence here suggests the most probable scenario for what happened to Mary Hankins that day. This explanation is still not definitive or absolute. But it is as close as anyone can come.

CHAPTER 12

1954 FINDINGS OF MAXINE CHESHIRE

After a year of researching, "Googling," and poring over old newspaper articles, a startling discovery was made. Maxine Cheshire, the award-winning reporter at the Washington Post during the '60's and '70's, had devoted two pages of her only book and autobiography, *Maxine Cheshire, Reporter* (with John Greenya), published in 1978, to the Hankins murder.

Ms. Cheshire, the former Maxine Hall, moved with her family from Harlan, Kentucky to Knoxville in the heat of an August night in 1951 to escape a threat to their safety, the kind of threat that was not an uncommon occurrence in Harlan in those days. She found work at *The Knoxville News-Sentinel* as a police beat reporter and honed her skills as an investigative reporter over the following three years. She also found the father of her children, Herb Cheshire, the United Press International bureau chief in Knoxville.

Maxine left Knoxville in November, 1954 following the transfer of her husband to Washington and joined the *Washington Post* as a "society reporter" (gossip columnist). She used the investigative skills she had learned in Knoxville to break stories that embarrassed and angered Washington politicians, First Ladies, and Hollywood celebrities.

Although the two final pages of the first chapter of Ms. Cheshire's book do not mention Mary Hankins or any suspects by name, the descriptions related make it clear to whom reference is being made. Ms. Cheshire described the victim of the murder as the "wealthy suburban wife of a well-known lumber company executive" who was murdered while her husband was gone to the store. According to the Knox County coroner, the victim was on her knees when she was shot. The husband was considered the primary suspect.

Ms. Cheshire received a tip that someone else was responsible and that she identified the killer through "a beat-up old car that had been seen parked on the street at the time of the murder." She interviewed the girlfriend of the killer who claimed to have been in the car at the time of the murder and had possession of the murder weapon. The boyfriend had several convictions for house-breaking and was incarcerated at the Brushy Mountain State Prison.

Ms. Cheshire further relates in her book that she spoke with the prosecuting attorney about the case and was informed that all the evidence in the case, including the slug that had been removed from the victim's head, had vanished when the new sheriff took office. Because of this, she was told by the prosecutor that the case would be impossible to prosecute.

Having an urge to see what the killer looked like, she made an appointment to see the warden at Brushy Mountain, and, in fact, had lunch with the warden in his office. When she got to the dessert, she found a note inside her apple turnover which read, "I know why you are here today. Guess who baked this? Guess what I could have put into it if I had wanted to?"

Ms. Cheshire, who had stayed behind a short period of time to cover this case when her husband left for Washington, decided to join her husband in Washington following her lunch with the warden.

Inasmuch as Ms. Cheshire's facts lack specificity and pertain to both of the suspects, Joseph Hegler and Bill Luallen, it appears that these pages were written over 20 years later from memory rather than from notes taken during her 3-year stint in Knoxville. There was no "beat-up old car" in the Hankins' neighborhood at the time of murder. The killer's girlfriend that she mentioned had to be Hegler's girlfriend, Jessie Waldrop. The suspect with house-breaking convictions who was incarcerated at Brushy Mountain and who could have baked the apple turnover describes Luallen.

Finally, the allegations that Sheriff Jones took all the evidence with him when he left office to prevent Sheriff Cate from solving the murder is not credible. Sheriff Jones made himself visible in offering his assistance after he was defeated by Sheriff Cate. It was reported that he was present in Chief Kinsey's office when Hegler was first interrogated. No such report was found when Luallen was interrogated by Sheriff Cate and his detectives.

There is little doubt that animosity existed between Cate and Kimsey and most likely, between Cate and Jones. There is no evidence, however, to support any allegation that this animosity extended to destruction or concealment of evidence in the Hankins case.

One vital piece of evidence that had to be available when Ms. Cheshire left Knoxville for Washington, D. C. in November 1954 was the murder weapon. Bill Luallen identified it as the revolver he stole from Andy Benton's Grocery.

CHAPTER 13

SUMMARY OF TRIAL EVIDENCE

As previously acknowledged, our justice system requires that a jury of our peers unanimously find guilt beyond a reasonable doubt. Applying this standard to the evidence against Bill Luallen for the murder of Mary Hankins, was there sufficient evidence to convict? Was the Knox County Attorney General's Office justified in not pursuing an indictment of Luallen in absence of a confession? Had the case been so botched due to ineptness and petty departmental jealousies that it precluded salvaging the evidence remaining and putting that evidence before a jury?

What follows is a list of the probable witnesses and their testimony as well as physical evidence that would have been presented at trial had Luallen been charged with Hankins' murder. It contains what is known and speculates to some degree as to the answers to some of the questions that were unanswered and/or unasked during the investigation.

C. Fred Hankins would have been called to testify to the activities of his wife and him on Saturday, March 31, 1951. His testimony would include how he found her when he returned home that afternoon and that the only item missing was her Gruen wristwatch.

Knox County Coroner Sidney Wolfenbarger would have testified as to the cause of Mrs. Hankins death and his opinion that she was on her knees when she was shot in the back of the head, which would have resulted in blood splatter on the shooter's mid-section.

Mary Elizabeth Schumaker, the Hankins' neighbor, would have testified concerning the man she saw enter the Hankins' home on that afternoon, including his description, his actions, his length of stay, and a description of the car he was driving.

Floyd Bruce, the convicted felon who was at the home of Buford Roberts at 5:00 p.m. the day of the murder, would have testified concerning Luallen's appearance when he arrived, including the blood on his shirt and pants, his lack of transportation, and why he was there. Bruce could also have possibly testified concerning Luallen's stealing a .32 caliber revolver shortly before the murder.

Buford Roberts could have been a witness or a defendant, or both, depending on the decisions made by the Attorney General and by Roberts. In 1954 Roberts was an inmate at Brushy Mountain where he was serving his sentence for accessory before the fact in the murder of Robert Grant in Roane County. He could have been charged with being an accessory after the fact in the murder of Mary Hankins in Knox County as he helped Luallen conceal evidence of the crime by transporting him to his mother's apartment in downtown Knoxville. Had he not been charged, he could have been granted immunity or called as a hostile witness. The goal of any such tactics on the part of the Attorney General would have been to solicit all information Roberts knew about this murder. Roberts' testimony, whether as a cooperating defendant or a hostile witness, would have served the prosecution well by placing him in a similar role in the Hankins murder that he had played in the Grant murder in which Luallen's older brother, Leon, was the shooter. Explaining Roberts' relationship with the

Luallen's would have explained why Bill Luallen came to Roberts' house the day of the murder for help.

John C. Johnson, the retired farmer from north Knox County, would have testified that he found the .32 Colt caliber revolver near Bull Run Creek off the Norris Freeway on June 17, 1951 and turned the gun over to Sheriff Jones the same day.

Sheriff C. W. "Buddy" Jones would have testified that he personally took the Colt revolver found by Johnson to the FBI Laboratory in Washington, D. C. and returned with it following the FBI's examination of the gun.

An expert witness from the FBI Laboratory would have testified of having concluded that the Colt revolver was the gun which fired the fatal slug taken from Mrs. Hankins head, and thus, establishing it was the murder weapon.

The witnesses and documentary evidence necessary to prove Luallen was arrested in a stolen 1950 Ford in Davenport, Iowa a week following the Hankins murder, and that he had purchased Campbell County, Tennessee tags for the car before noon on the day of the murder would have been presented.

The witnesses and documentary evidence necessary to establish Luallen's *modus operandi* in committing daytime house burglaries and the kinds of items he had taken in previous such burglaries would have been presented.

The witnesses and documentary evidence necessary to establish Luallen's escape status between February 9 and April 6, 1951 would have been presented.

Knox County Sheriff's Detective Pat Patterson, and any other officers as necessary, would have testified to Luallen's admission that he stole the murder weapon from

Andy Benton's Grocery in Andersonville prior to the murder.

The above listed witnesses and evidence in this mock trial are not all-inclusive. Invariably, additional witnesses and evidence of significance come to light during the course of most trials, but the evidence listed represents the meat of the case. Whether this case would have satisfied the reasonable doubt standard is not known. This is only a question that a jury can decide, and this case never went to a jury.

Of course, consideration has to be given to what might have come from the other side of the aisle – from the defense. The evidence offered to establish the timeline, albeit circumstantial, makes the establishment of an alibi difficult and circumspect. Who would have gotten on the witness stand to vouch for Luallen's whereabouts at the time of the murder? He was an escapee driving a stolen car. Who would have furnished him an alibi? Perhaps his mother. No one else comes to mind. How effective could any alibi witness have been? Defending this case with an alibi witness would have been extremely difficult.

Offering a defense to this case, alibi or other, would have been next to impossible. The only defense would have been to try to discredit the State's witnesses and to argue reasonable doubt. The defense would only have been as good as the lawyer representing the defendant, and it is unlikely Ray Jenkins would have been that lawyer since he had prosecuted Leon Luallen and Buford Roberts in Roane County the year before. No, the defense would have been in a very precarious, unenviable position.

Aside from not having a viable defense, the defense would not have had a viable defendant. Bill Luallen had never gone to trial on any charges. He had always entered guilty pleas and served his time. This case would have been different. He could have been facing a death penalty, not a few months back at Brushy Mountain, then out, then back again like a revolving door. Luallen's arrogance and cocky demeanor would not have bode well for him in the courtroom, and he would have been difficult for his lawyer to advise or control. He had displayed his arrogance and contempt for the law over the years in many ways. In 1944 he had alleged his ex-wife, Wynona, committed the 1943 murder of Maoma Ridings in Indianapolis, then a week later recanted and falsely confessed to the murder himself. Before escaping from the Loudon County work camp seven weeks before the Hankins murder, Luallen boasted that he was going to break his older brother, Leon, out of the Roane County Jail. Any defense attorney would have had his hands full representing Bill Luallen.

Regrettably, a Knox County jury was never afforded the opportunity to hear the evidence, consider the defense, or observe Bill Luallen in the courtroom.

EPILOGUE

During the course of the investigative research for this book, which entailed not only documentary evidence but interview of family members and friends, it became painfully evident that the shadow of suspicion cast by the 1951 Knoxville newspapers concerning the victim's family and that of her husband, was unfounded. Unjustly, without the opportunity for public rebuttal, the families were put in a light that reflected a warped and inaccurate portrait of these people. All families have disputes, but most don't commit murder to resolve them. Neither did the Hankins or the Tablers. Just talking to family and friends gave the author a feel for the caliber of these people. If that had been done in 1951 a different portrait might have been painted and the suspicion created could have been erased rather than perpetuated.

The murder of Mary Hankins was an impetuous crime committed by a desperate man. It was not an act committed by a family member for a motive that never existed.

James William Luallen walked out of Brushy Mountain State Prison on July 4, 1965 and never returned to the Tennessee Prison system. He died in Nashville on August 30, 1982. His obituary in *The Nashville Tennessean* listed survivors as one daughter, Mary Joyce Luallen of Virginia; three brothers, Otha Hunley of Lake City, Leon Luallen of Nashville, and Roy Luallen of Indiana; four sisters, Mrs. Mary Proctor of Florida, Betty Sue Luallen of Knoxville, Mrs. Bessie Thompson and Mrs. Virginia Robinson, both of California. The service was held at a Nashville funeral home but he was buried at Woodlawn Cemetery in Knoxville with his parents and his brother, Jack Brownlow Luallen.

One final comment is made for the record. Extensive efforts were made to locate and interview a living relative of James William Luallen. A nephew was tentatively located who could have helped, but no response was received. Four different addresses were developed for this nephew, the son of Leon Luallen. Letters soliciting the nephew's help and cooperation were mailed to each of the four addresses during June and July, 2010. Two of the letters were returned by the Postal Service; two were not.

In addition, considerable time was spent in an effort to locate Luallen's daughter, Mary Joyce Luallen, listed in his obituary as residing in Virginia, however, no address or other identifiable information enabling her location was developed. Neither was her mother's identity determined. Luallen was believed to have only been married once, this being to Wynona Yoe in 1940, however, they divorced in 1944. Luallen had "Hazel" tattooed between his right thumb and index finger, but this person's identity was not determined.

ACKNOWLEDGEMENTS

Grateful acknowledgements are given to Retha Dalton Hankins, whom Fred Hankins married nine years after the death of Mary, and her twin sister, Letha Dalton Wilkins, for their generosity in sharing information and the Hankins family photographs depicted in the introduction and the first chapter.

BIBLIOGRAPHY

Articles

Aimes, E. V. "Three Shots for Help—How Many for Murder?" *Official Detectives Stories,* March 1952

Layne, Hugh. "Bellyfull of Murder." *Inside Detective,* July 1950

Books

Cheshire, Maxine, and John Greenya, *Maxine Cheshire, Reporter.* Boston: Houghton Mifflin Company, 1978

1951 Knoxville Central High School Yearbook

Internet

Ancestry.com

cases/justia.com/us-court-of-appeals

peoplefinders.com

pixelp.com/gruen

Wikipedia, The Free Encyclopedia

Newspapers

Dixon Evening Telegraph (Dixon, Illinois)

Kingsport Times

Mansfield News-Journal (Mansfield, Ohio)

Middlesboro Daily News (Middlesboro, Kentucky)

Monroe County Observer (Madisonville, Tennessee)

The Brownsville Herald (Brownsville, Texas)

The Democrat & Leader (Davenport, Iowa)

The Dothan Eagle (Dothan, Alabama)

The Harriman Record (Harriman, Tennessee)

The Knoxville Journal

The Knoxville News-Sentinel

The Nashville Tennessean

The Progress-Index (Petersburg, Virginia)

The News-Palladium (Benton Harbor, Michigan)

The Vidette Messenger (Valparaiso, Indiana)

The Zanesville Signal (Zanesville, Ohio)

Public Records

City of Knoxville Mayor's Office

Knox County Sheriff's Office

Roane County, Tennessee, Archives

State of Tennessee Department of Correction

Made in the USA
Middletown, DE
09 December 2023

45062967R00066